HOW TO
DEMOCRAT
IN THE AGE OF TRUMP

MIKE LUX

STRONG
ARM
PRESS

WASHINGTON D.C.

Requests for permission to reproduce selections from this book should be mailed to: Strong Arm Press, 1440 G St NW, Washington, D.C. 20005

Published in the United States by Strong Arm Press, 2018

www.strongarmpress.com

Book Composition by Strong Arm Press.

ISBN-13: 978-1-947492-13-4
ISBN: 1-947492-13-6

Praise for *How To Democrat In the Age of Trump*

"Few people understand the American left as well as Mike Lux. Only someone with his deep roots in progressive action could write a book this smart, this timely and this important. If you care about where the country is headed, you should read every page."
-Raul Grijalva

"Mike Lux has given us a thought-provoking and practical guide with an important message: promoting a bold progressive vision to expand economic opportunity will resonate with every American. If we come together around that vision — and follow Lux's wise advise — Democrats will win and our country will win."
-Jan Schakowsky

"Mike Lux argues that Democrats need to return to a core message aimed at working class families, Black, Brown and White. Fighting Trump can't be the primary focus for our political work. Progressive means forward ever on economic and social justice, not simply opposition."
-Larry Cohen, Board Chair Our Revolution, former President, Communications Workers of America

"Mike Lux draws on his decades of experience fighting for progressive causes and his rare insider's view of the Democratic Party to give us an incisive analysis of the Party's recent failures and a clear and inspiring path back to durable governing power. His forceful argument for the Democrats to return to their roots as the party of the people - on the side of the working class and those fighting for freedom from injustice - needs to be heard and heeded. His message to grassroots forces outside the beltway that our time is coming if we're willing to do the messy work of politics is right on time."
-Deepak Bhargava, Center for Community Change Action

"To go from Resistance to resurgence and resurgence to renewal, we don't need pundits and pollsters to show the way. We need progressive populist organizers like Mike Lux, a guy who not only knows what it means to be a Democrat but how to win tough elections across America. This book ignites the conversation we need to have in the Democratic Party."
-Jamie Raskin

"Mike Lux speaks the hard truth to all progressive candidates interested in winning elections. You can not and should not ignore rural voters. A progressive economic agenda can and should be the roadmap to increased family incomes, expanded access to quality health care, and an improved infrastructure."
-Tom Vilsack, former Iowa Governor and Secretary of Agriculture in the Obama administration

"*How To Democrat in the Age of Trump* is a must read for anyone who cares about the future of the Democratic Party."
-Joel Silberman, President, Media Talent 2.0

CONTENTS

NOTES AND ACKNOWLEDGEMENTS

Writing a book on Democratic Party strategy in this particular moment of American history is fraught with tension. When I told one friend I was doing it, he said, "Wow, how does it feel to be walking through a minefield?" I know everyone who reads this book will no doubt have strong opinions on everything I will say, so it will be a wild ride. Additionally, because I have friends in a lot of different sectors of the Democratic Party, and I do not religiously adhere to any one dogma, I'm sure I will be hearing a lot of grumbling from my friends. Apologies to all in advance if I piss you off too badly. I hope not to burn any bridges beyond repair. That is certainly not my intent, but one never knows how folks will react.

The idea for this book has been marinating in my brain for a long time now, but the advent of the Trump era spurred me on more than ever. When my old friends Alex Lawson and Ryan Grim started Strong Arm Press, an idea formed in my head. Strong Arm is a progressive publishing house that can turn books around and publish them quickly, as opposed to the yearlong process typically required by a traditional publishing house. I got inspired and cut a deal with them early this year to get this book out this spring. For one thing, in times like these, so much is going on so quickly that writing a political book with a long lead time doesn't make much sense. But in addition, the hope was to have a book that could stir up some debate in the party leading up to the 2018 elections, and be the opening salvo in the 2020 cycle about what kind of presidential campaign we should be running. Strong Arm has been a wonderful partner to work with on this project.

Our decision to move this quickly on the book means there will be some things we missed -- important data, analysis, and ideas we left out, as well as the little typos and sentence glitches you will no doubt find here. Apologies for those errors.

Whenever a political party comes away with a loss in an election, there is a lot of soul searching, as there should be. But when you lose an election everyone is expecting you to win, and you lose it to one of the most repulsive men in the history of the country, the post-mortems are brutal -- again, as they should be. Fortunately, even in the midst of all the blame-gaming and handwringing, there are some really constructive ideas and projects

i

that emerge. I want to note three of the most important ones, all of which had an influence on my thinking as I wrote this book.

The first project was one that my colleague Lauren Windsor and I have been involved in from the beginning. As the smoke cleared from the 2016 debacle, and people shifted from being obsessed with the presidential results and started thinking about how much we had cumulatively been losing over the last decade, it was evident that the very word 'Democrat,' the brand and definition of the party itself, was badly damaged. A diverse group of leaders from across the party informally came together to explore ways of "Rebuilding Democrat" as a concept. We did a lot of research which strongly indicated that Democrats had an opportunity to capture the hijacked word of freedom from the right-wing and that voters did have some trust in Democrats to build a better future for their families. We also came to the conclusion that a focus on fairness and the future are two essential concepts that would create a clear contrast with Republicans and Trump.

Having been involved in a lot of different discussions of what the Democratic brand, message, identity, slogan, etc. should be over the last quarter century, most of which turned straight into mush, I was impressed by this project. The research and thinking that went into it is reflected strongly in this book.

A second new project I want to mention is called Dem Labs. It was the brainchild of my friend Donnie Fowler, who is mentioned multiple times in this book. The idea of Dem Labs was to bring together some of the best people from the worlds of art/entertainment, politics, and technology to germinate solutions to problems facing the party. Discussions focused on how to give Democratic candidates at all levels, especially the local level where far too little attention has been paid, the tools they needed to run modern campaigns and tell compelling stories. Donnie asked me to be one of several people organizing three conferences, two in SF and one in NYC. After the conferences were over, ideas continued to develop, and Dem Labs started coming up with new tools and ideas for campaigns. The whole process was invaluable, and the emphasis on local campaigns and building from the ground up is right on track.

Finally, I want to mention my friend of 35 years, Mike Podhorzer, who is the political director of the AFL-CIO. Mike has started pulling together a couple hundred political strategists from a wide variety of sectors in the Democratic Party for discussions and panel presentations on different aspects of winning campaigns. Every weekend he sends us the latest in new research and analysis on electoral trends and tactics. It is invaluable to be a part of this community Mike has built. He shares a wealth of data with us, and some of this info and analysis is reflected in the book.

Mike also was kind enough to be one of the first people to review my very earliest rough draft of this book, and the suggestions he gave me, many of which went very deep, were profoundly helpful.

I want to acknowledge a few other people who have influenced me a great deal in how I am thinking about politics. The first is Mark Riddle, the head of the New Leaders Council, and one of the key movers and shakers behind the "Rebuilding Democrat" project mentioned above. He has been a big influence as I think about the way forward.

Leo Hindery, whom I mention in the book, has been a stalwart friend and supporter in many different endeavors over the past 20 years. He is many different things: a successful businessman and investor, a philanthropist to a bunch of great causes, a major donor and fundraiser for progressive candidates, and an author. But most surprising of all for the people who know him only by reputation, he is an issue wonk of the first magnitude. He loves digging into the details of issues to get good things done that help people.

My colleagues in Democracy Partners are a sprawling and diverse collection of progressive consultants who have been involved for years in all manner of left-of-center politics, sometimes inside the Democratic Party and sometimes for progressive causes. In weekly calls and quarterly meetings, they share information and insights about what is happening politically around the country. Those discussions are invaluable, and have shaped many of my ideas about political strategy. I want to take author's prerogative and tell you all their names: Aaron Black, Heather Booth, Marc Cerabona, Wyatt Closs, Robert Creamer, Mac D'Alessandro, Brett C. Di Resta, A'shanti Gholar, Daniel Gouldman, Ken Grossinger, David Grossman, John Hennelly,

Marilyn Katz, Jackie Kendall, Gebe Martinez, Josie Mooney, Patrick Pannett, Khalid Pitts, Marvin Randolph, Joe Sandler, Linda Saucedo, Renee Schaeffer, Joel Silberman, Cheri Whiteman, and Lauren Windsor.

Some partners of course I am particularly close to.

Heather Booth is a legend in the world of progressive organizing, starting with her activism in Mississippi Summer in 1964. She has been a trusted mentor and dear friend for almost 40 years, from the time when she met me at the age of 20 and said, "I'm looking for people who are willing to make a life-long commitment to the progressive movement." Once I said yes, I was in for good because I could not break my promise to her.

I've known Bob Creamer, whose office is next door to mine, almost as long. He and his wife, Jan Schakowsky, who is a congresswoman from Illinois, have provided me so much great guidance over the years. Jan's chief of staff, Cathy Hurwit, has also been a dear friend and big influence.

Marvin Randolph teaches me innovative new ways to motivate people of color to vote practically every time I talk to him. He is one of the best field organizers I have ever known.

And my dear friend, Joel Silberman, whose career has spanned from being a performer and producer in the arts to training progressive politicians and media personalities, has been a strategic and funny guide to how media is working in the age of Trump. Joel has been fighting cancer while I have been writing this book, and his unquenchable spirit and determination in the face of that battle is an inspiration every day.

In terms of key people on Capitol Hill, the friendship, political and policy ideas, and support of several important legislators and their chiefs of staff should be noted, including Elizabeth Warren and Dan Geldon; Sherrod Brown and Sarah Benzing; Jeff Merkley and Mike Zamore; Keith Ellison and Donna Cassutt; and Raul Grijalva and Amy Emerick Clerkin. Gabi Lemus, who is the president of the foundation working closely with the Congressional Progressive Caucus, has been a good friend on the Hill for many years as well.

I also want to thank my family back home in Nebraska. My two brothers, two sisters, and I were raised by parents and grandparents who cared deeply about their neighbors, their community, and the world around them. They raised us to care about human decency and dignity, to treat others with kindness -- the way we would want to be treated -- and to be generous to those who needed a helping hand. We have a huge family, among them teachers, preachers, artists, social workers, health care workers and parents who make the world a better place. My most basic ideas about what politics at its best should be about, and my passion for making a difference in the world, come from my family.

Finally, this book would never have been written without the major assistance of three remarkable women.

Andrea Haverdink, our firm's associate producer, has been an employee for about a year and a half. Before that she was one of the best interns ever for two summers in a row. Usually her production work is more on the video side; she partners with Lauren Windsor to produce most of the online videos for Mike Lux Media (MLM) and American Family Voices (AFV). She works with me closely to put out a political analysis web-show called Mike Lux, The Politics Guy. Much of the humor and fun of that series comes from her contribution of graphics and pop culture references.

For the book, Andrea became our chief fact checker. This assignment was a particularly challenging job, because my brain has all kinds of facts squirreled away in various places -- dates in history, polling percentages, vote totals from campaigns, going back 40 years. I don't always remember, however, where these facts came from. So the fact-checking not only involved whether my memory was correct (I'm happy to say it mostly was), but also finding a solid source for each number. It was a huge undertaking, and Andrea did a wonderful job of getting it all done and then organizing everything for the bibliography at the back of the book.

Lauren Windsor has been my colleague and one of my best friends for almost five years now. She has been our leading video producer for MLM and AFV, and has her own web news show, The Undercurrent, which has broken several big stories in recent years, including exposing one of the Koch brothers' secretive donor retreats. She has also become the leading expert in the country on the ugly tactics of Project Veritas. Lauren has a wicked sense of humor, is one of the gutsiest and most doggedly determined people I have ever known, is brilliant and creative as all get-out, and takes no shit from anyone.

Lauren's passion about climate change and money in politics helped drive the writing in those areas. Her insights about Democrats being the party of the future, contrasted to the MAGA-centric, backward-looking Republicans, were critical to my thinking, and her ideas about freedom were another foundational part of the book.

Lauren has been one of my two editors, adding some substantive narrative and offering me many good strategic ideas. She reminds me every day that people younger than me have an enormous -- and very healthy -- skepticism about the conventional wisdom of my generation, and that it is a good thing to shake up the establishment in D.C. on a very regular basis. Not just in the writing of this book, but ever since we became friends, she has given me a ton of great ideas about politics, has challenged me to open up my thinking, and has inspired me to keep fighting the good fight. She regularly lends her business skills (better than mine) to our operation and has taken on extra project work as I write this book, so I am grateful to her for that well.

The final person I want to thank is my other editor, my wife, Barbara Laur. She was the main editor on my first book as well, and on a great many things I have written over the 37 wonderful years we have been together, in addition to all the other incredible things she does for me every day. She knows my voice, knows my heart, and (usually) knows what I mean when I write strange meandering run-on sentences that don't make sense. Not being in the world of politics for a career, she can tell me when I'm using jargon that won't play with regular folks. She is always my best check on decency and basic common sense. Being a farmer's daughter, she was also a good check on the rural culture and values I wrote about in the book.

I am inspired by ideas and by the values I was raised on. I am inspired even more by the people I work with every day in the progressive movement and Democratic Party. But no one will ever inspire me more than Barbara, the foundation I build my life upon. Without her, I know this book would never have been written, because I would probably be babbling to myself on a street corner somewhere. She is the love of my life, which makes me a very lucky man indeed.

PROLOGUE

We have the most dangerous, corrupt, erratic, openly racist and sexist president this country has ever had. And in part because we failed at the top of the ticket, but even more because Democrats have had a flawed political strategy over the last decade, both houses of Congress are now run by the most far-right party in modern history as well.

This book is about how we fix the mess we are in politically and start winning elections again on a sustained basis. Just as importantly, it is also about how we come back from this terrible moment and revitalize the Democratic Party. Even if we win in 2018, even if we win the presidency in 2020, if we don't build a Democratic Party that will succeed in creating a sustained progressive era that will lift up our country up, we will almost immediately start losing again. And every time we lose, the consequences to our country, already terrible, will continue to worsen. Donald Trump is a symptom, not the cause, of our political failure, and we need a new progressive era to wash the stink away.

At its heart, this book is about the intersection of class, race, and politics, because the crash we have had is at that intersection. The good news is that we have a road out of the wilderness if only we choose to take it. I want to begin this book by telling a story of hope.

A local Minnesota coalition called Our Minnesota Future recently partnered with a national progressive think tank called

Demos Action, and researchers including the firm Brilliant Corners, Celinda Lake, Ian Haney López, and Anat Shenker-Osorio in a groundbreaking study with results that Democrats need to understand and internalize. (Anat and Celinda are good friends of mine who have been on the cutting edge of linguistics and progressive messaging research, and Demos has been an ally, all for many years.)

In the research project, Our Minnesota Future did door-to-door canvassing of 800 homes. Half of these conversations at the doors were with white folks, the other half were with people of color. They showed these folks flyers that used what the researchers called "classic dog whistling"- traditional Republican rhetoric about the economy combined with attacks on immigrants and racial undertones. After seeing that Republican rhetoric, 50% of the people at the doors were shown flyers with a traditional progressive populist message on the economy, while the other 50% were shown a flyer with a progressive race-class narrative. The latter said the following:

> Whether white, black, or brown, 5th generation or newcomer, we all want to build a better future for our children. My opponent says some families have value, while others don't count. He wants to pit us against each other in order to gain power for himself and kickbacks for his donors.

The majority of white survey participants initially agreed with the dog whistle flyer. When shown the class-only populist flyer, 44% of them shifted to the progressive candidate, but a 55% majority did not. The results were inverse for whites who were shown the other flyer that combined economic populism and a "they are trying to divide us by race" analysis: 57% went to the progressive candidate, while 43% stuck with the conservative.

Meanwhile, when the doorknockers talked to people of color, surprisingly, a plurality initially agreed with the dog whistle script. Sixty-two percent of these minority respondents switched to the progressive candidate after being shown the combined race-class messaging.

Finally, researchers investigated one other thing among people of color: motivation to vote. When shown the class-only progressive populist flyer, the people of color surveyed were twice as likely to sit out the election than when shown the race-class messaging.

In addition to the canvassing, Celinda (who a lot of us think of as the ethical Frank Luntz of the left) conducted polling to test what narratives worked the best in comparison to more traditional messaging approaches. Her advice coming out of that testing was in line with the Minnesota experiment: discuss race up front and overtly. Frame racism as a tool to divide and thus harm us all for the benefit of a few. Connect unity to both racial justice and economic prosperity.

This is just one experiment, but it reinforces what I have become convinced of after all my years in politics: it is a bad idea to avoid challenging topics with voters. The most challenging, central, and foundational of all is racism, and Democrats can't avoid it, ignore it, not bring it up, or hope it will go away. It's bad morally, but it's also bad strategically. The people of color and progressive whites who support us will turn away from the party if we try to avoid this subject. The way to win is to tie racism and economics directly together, and to educate and organize in both communities of color and white, working-class folks.

I write this book as a longtime political warrior who has seen the good, the bad, and the ugly of Democratic politics up close and personal. I started out in the early 1980s, as a family farm, community, and labor organizer in Nebraska and Iowa, rural blue collar states with lots of Republicans, but also places where I saw strong progressive messages break through and win. I've worked on the inside of half a dozen presidential campaigns, was a senior adviser to the DNC the last two months before the 2016 election, worked on both of the Democratic presidential transition teams in my adulthood, and was a special assistant to the president in the Clinton White House.

I came to D.C. with the Clintons. I worked in the legendary 1992 Clinton campaign war room in Little Rock; the 1993 White House war room where we got the Clinton economic plan passed by the skin of our teeth; and the ill-fated "delivery room" that tried and failed to get health care reform passed in 1994. I was one of only two people (Gene Sperling was the other) who worked in all three. This book has its share of blunt criticisms of the political and policy mistakes made by the Clintons, and those of us who worked for them, in the '90s and in the 2016 campaign. Notwithstanding those criticisms, I will always be grateful to the Clintons for bringing me to the White House, and I will always believe many of the things we did were good things that helped the American people.

Once I left the White House, I did some establishment Democratic things, too: running independent expenditure ad campaigns, raising money and helping on various political projects for Democratic candidates and party committees, and playing an early role in helping John Podesta found the Center for American Progress.

So if you are a progressive outsider who thinks all of us in D.C. are corrupt, you can definitely cast me as an evil D.C. insider. But I've also always been a part of the outsider progressive movement as well. I gave an assist to Wes Boyd and Joan Blades when they started MoveOn.org. Wes called me "the very first insider to notice MoveOn." In late 2001 when the Enron scandal created a moment to organize around corporate responsibility, I started one of the very first blogs on politics and policy, something called The Daily Enron. (We published every day for a year at the height of that controversy.) Later on, I brought the insider's voice to an influential little blog called Open Left that I initiated with my partners Chris Bowers and Matt Stoller, two of the most brilliant pioneers on the progressive blogosphere.

In the mid-aughts, I helped create a long-term strategic plan for the immigration reform movement that launched an organizational infrastructure that remains in place today. In 2008, I helped write the strategic plan and fundraise for the progressive coalition Health Care for America Now, the organization that pushed Obama from the left on health care and helped get the ACA passed. I also played a role in helping create and fund Americans for Financial Reform, the outside coalition led by my friend and business partner Heather Booth, that worked with Elizabeth Warren to get Dodd-Frank and the Consumer Financial Protection Bureau written into law. (By the way, they won that fight even though they were outspent by about 500-1.) I have been a co-founder and fundraiser for several new progressive organizations, but what I am most proud of is having been a mentor to a large number of progressive activists who are rising stars in our movement, several of whom will be mentioned in this book.

Through all of this work, I have gotten to see American politics from many different angles. Dysfunction, cynicism, and corruption have become the rule of the day. I've watched our political discourse become more and more dysfunctional, and more and more angry. The dynamic between the political parties has gotten more poisoned for sure, but this degree of animus is not just between the parties, but between the Democratic Party and the progressive movement. I have always been a bridge-builder and coalition-builder between people who didn't know or understand each other very well, but I increasingly feel like a lot of my old friends just flat out hate each other.

My career has been situated on the bridge between the progressive movement and the Democratic Party establishment. Now, amidst our most urgent crisis, with our democratic form of government and the rule of law in the balance, that bridge is feeling pretty damn rickety. I believe with all my heart that unless we repair it, it will get swept away by the storm, and that would be a tragedy because we can't beat the Republicans without a unified Democratic Party.

I believe that the only thing that will ultimately solve our nation's political problems is for Democrats to reclaim the mantle of the party of the people, start winning elections again, and then actually deliver tangible benefits that the American people can see, feel, and understand. We have to prove to people that government, when it is actually on the side of the people and not big money special interests, can be effective in delivering a better quality of life for them and their families.

I don't for a minute believe there is anything simple or easy about getting this done. I have no naiveté about achieving a kumbaya moment between the warring factions of our party. Because I don't believe in easy answers, and because everyone I know FEELS VERY STRONGLY ABOUT EVERYTHING, I go into the enterprise of writing this book on Democratic strategy knowing full well that probably every single person who reads it will find some things in it they disagree with at least a little. What I hope, though, is that it opens up a genuine dialogue between people of good faith, that it provokes discussion and maybe even some honest give-and-take as to how we get through the ugly morass we are in right now as a party and a country.

If there is one message I want to convey to the leaders of the Democratic Party, it is that we have to recognize that we will never win by ignoring or dismissing the passions and ideas of the activists who animate our own grassroots. We cannot win from the top down, making most of the major decisions sitting in front of computer screens in D.C., ignoring the voices of the local activists who are our heart and soul. And we can't win by spending more of our attention on making high-dollar funders happy than we do with our voters, activists, and small-dollar donors. We have to acknowledge that the base of our party -- people of color, young people, unmarried working-class women, poor people -- have not been well-served economically by the American government for a couple of generations now, through Democratic as well as Republican administrations, and we need to pay attention to why they are angry. The party's future is with the grassroots, and if our grassroots activists are not happy, we need to do something about it.

And if there is one message I want to send to my progressive grassroots friends outside the D.C. power centers, it is this: your time is coming, but politics is messy and complicated -- and that's okay. There's not much in politics that is either pure evil, or pure goodness and light. You shouldn't accept what the experts and insiders say, because you are just as likely, maybe more likely, as they are to be right. But also understand what one of my most important mentors in politics, Paul Tully, taught me long ago: you can't take the politics out of politics. There is nothing pure or simple or easy about political work, but that doesn't make it all dirty. To get anything done in the political realm, you have to compromise, you've got to be willing to engage in give-and-take, you have to cajole and maneuver and persuade, not just demand. And by the way, all that messiness is beautiful, not bad. It builds organizations and forges bonds; it makes democratic governance possible.

For those of you so alienated by the Democrats that you think that they are just the same as the Republicans, or you think that politics doesn't matter, or is too corrupt to participate in, you may hesitate to listen to what this old-timer has to say. But I got into politics, and I remain in politics today, to make poor and working-class people's lives better. I can tell you this: the only time in my 40 years in issue organizing I have ever seen any progress at all in America was when enough Democrats got elected to push through positive change. Yeah, there were way too many things that didn't get done, and some big policy mistakes along the way. But since I've been in politics, when they have had the political power, Democrats have:

- ended Reagan's war in Central America in the 1980s by cutting off appropriations;
- passed the Americans with Disabilities Act;
- increased the minimum wage three times at the national level and in states and cities across the country;
- raised taxes on the wealthy substantially, twice at the national level and in many states and localities around the country, and lowered taxes for the poor through the Earned Income Tax Credit;
- passed a Family and Medical Leave law;
- expanded children's health care to cover more than nine million children;
- expanded Medicaid coverage dramatically;
- prohibited insurance companies from discriminating against people with pre-existing conditions;
- expanded the National Park System massively;
- created the Consumer Financial Protection Bureau, and tightened other important regulatory measures on Wall Street;
- joined 194 other countries in the Paris Climate Agreement to commit to reducing carbon emissions; and
- joined an international coalition to keep Iran from developing nuclear weapons.

Just as importantly, Democrats have stopped some of the most terrible things Republicans keep trying to do. Social Security, Medicare, Medicaid, and public education are all still here because Democrats stopped Republicans from destroying them.

This is important stuff, folks. To the tens of millions of Americans whose lives got saved by access to health care, or whose wages got increased for the first time in years, or who got money back from a bank that had cheated them, or who got to stay home with a sick kid, this matters in a big way. Anyone who dismisses these successes because we didn't get everything we wanted, doesn't understand the importance of policy in changing real people's lives.

The thing about having Democrats in power is that it makes progress possible. Not automatic, in any sense of the word. Not easy, ever. Not as much as we would want, ever. But possible: it opens up the fight for change, rather than politics just being about fighting off the latest impending harm.

One final note: I know that as I write this in the spring of 2018, the Democratic Party has good reason to feel optimistic about the elections this fall. We have been doing really well in special elections and other off-year elections so far this cycle, as the Republican Party base is divided and a little discouraged, and Democratic base voters are turning out in good numbers. As one waggish friend of mine says, Democrats haven't been this optimistic since October, 2016.

All of this may still be the case in November, and it may not. My argument is that it is precisely because the potential is so great, and precisely because we have fallen short of expectations so many times in the recent past, that there is no time like the present to have a deep reassessment of our strategies to make sure we are on track. To lose the opportunity we now possess, or to have one good election cycle and then think all our problems are solved, would be a tragedy beyond repair.

INTRODUCTION

Our nation's future hangs on a precipice. A nasty man named Donald Trump is our president and Congress is controlled by the most extreme right-wing version of the Republican Party in our country's history. There are terrible consequences to millions of people happening as a result. I feel an obligation to fight this ugliness up close and personal every day.

Yet in spite of the seriousness of what we face, I write this book with the hope that we can once again overcome. The Trump administration has provoked a higher level of engaged progressive activism than I have ever seen in my 40 years of political work, and even some Republicans are reacting with dismay to this presidency. I see hopeful signs in the election results of the first 18 months of Trump's term in office.

Most importantly, in the long narrative of our nation's history, people facing far worse odds -- people literally enslaved, people with no votes or economic power -- overcame their oppression and rebuilt a society far better than the one they inherited. The Dred Scott decision was closely followed by the abolition of slavery. Decades of Big Business owning our government lock, stock, and barrel led us to the progressive reforms of the early 1900s and 1930s. McCarthyism and the Jim Crow violence of the 1950s were followed by the progress of the 1960s.

It is within our power, following this dark moment, to write a story of rebirth and renewal of the American Dream just as inspiring to the generations that follow us. This book will spell out how people of good will can start winning again.

But first, we need to spend a little time looking at how we got to where we are right now, and that is going to be a little depressing.

A decade ago, Democrats were flourishing and looked to be in the catbird seat for some time to come. They had just elected the first black president ever, son of an African immigrant with an African-Muslim name, with a 53% majority (the highest percentage for a Democratic presidential candidate since the LBJ landslide in 1964, and the second highest since the FDR glory years in the 1930s and '40s). They had the biggest margin in the House since the early 1990s, and 60 votes in the Senate for the first time since the late 1970s. They had the majority of governorships and all the state level constitutional offices such as lieutenant governorships, secretaries of state, attorneys general, and treasurers. They controlled the majority of state legislative chambers that would determine redistricting.

On top of all that, both demographics and issues seemed to be moving in the Democrats' favor. The demographic groups that tended to support the party (African-Americans, Latinos, other people of color, unmarried women, the religiously unaffiliated, and millennials) were all growing as a percentage of the population, while Republican-leaning demographic groups (older, whiter, more religious, married, and rural folks) were shrinking. More people were moving into cities because of a new vitality in the urban core of America, and when they moved, they tended to become more liberal.

Meanwhile, Republican control of government for most of the past decade, combined with the financial crash of 2008, had left big majorities of voters completely disillusioned with trickle-down economics and deregulatory frenzies. Voters were ready for a big change, and with sweeping control of every branch of the government, Democrats looked poised to give it to them.

While voters had some concerns about Democrats, if you went down the list of issues they were most concerned about, their viewpoints mostly mirrored the Democratic Party's public positioning. Imposing higher taxes for the wealthy and closing corporate loopholes; enacting tougher regulations on Wall Street; increasing the minimum wage; mandating paid family and medical leave; expanding Social Security, Medicare, Medicaid, and health care coverage; supporting public education and easing student debt;

strengthening civil rights, abortion rights, and LGBT rights; reforming immigration; and fighting climate change and environmental destruction were among the wide array of issues on which large majorities of voters firmly agreed with most Democrats. Ten years later, they still do, and in many cases in even stronger numbers.

Democrats looked like they were setting themselves up for what I called in my first book, *The Progressive Revolution: How the Best in America Came to Be*, another 'Big Change Moment.' Big Change Moments are the periods in American history when the country makes major policy strides in the direction of progress. The Big Change Moments I cited in The Progressive Revolution were the 1860s, led by Lincoln and the Radical Republicans (they were radical in a different way back then); the Progressive era of the early 1900s; the New Deal era of the 1930s and '40s; and the 1960s. These were eras of monumental progressive change that made the country a far better place.

I believed that if the Democrats delivered this kind of Big Change Moment, combined with all the demographic and political trends cited above, they would succeed in winning a multi-decade run similar to the New Deal era as the long-term majority party in this country. I am still convinced that this new golden era would have happened if Democrats had been more brave: if bolder structural reforms like a strong public option for health care and breaking up the Too-Big-to-Fail Wall Street banks had been passed; if the Wall Street executives who had caused the financial crisis had been prosecuted and sent to jail; and if President Obama had played hardball with Republicans in a variety of negotiations and witch-hunts aimed at his administration. (Somehow he believed that he could negotiate in good faith with a Republican Party bent on making him a one-term president at any cost.)

Ultimately, President Obama and the Democrats failed to deliver the Big Change Moment that our country needed, and we have been paying the price for that failure.

We also have been paying the price for too many of our party's leaders blindly accepting a set of old beliefs about how you win in politics that no longer fit the way voters think or make decisions in today's world. These Democrats adhere to formulas that worked at times in the 1990s and earlier -- that the key swing voters are well-to-do, economically moderate white voters who live in the suburbs and that TV ads are the main way to influence voters. But neither makes much sense these days as a political strategy.

Instead of a sustained political majority, none of the expected political success for Democrats happened. Obama did win re-election in 2012, and through two more election cycles we managed to hang onto control of the Senate. But the overall record for the last decade has been the worst electoral run for the Democratic Party since the post-Civil War years.

In the decade since our 2008 peak, when the future looked so promising, we have lost a net 11 U.S. Senate seats, 12 governorships, 63 U.S. House seats, control of 32 state legislative chambers, and 903 state legislative seats (and that's after we picked up 36 seats in Virginia, New Jersey, and special elections in 2017). We also, in case you hadn't noticed, lost the presidency in 2016, to the least prepared and most polarizing demagogue perhaps ever.

That's a hell of a lot of losing, folks.

The bulk of these losses came in two of the worst electoral blowouts in modern history, the massive Republican tidal waves in 2010 and 2014. The first tidal wave in 2010 allowed the Republicans to completely control the once-a-decade redistricting process in many states in 2011. This exacerbated the losses in the 2014 wipeout and kept Democratic gains to a minimum even in 2012, our best election of the decade. The states where Republicans controlled both houses of the legislature and the governor's office also passed the infamous set of voter suppression laws which have made voting more difficult for poor people, young people, and people of color. These laws contributed to many Republican victories in the years since.

But even if you take into account redistricting and voter suppression, even if you factor in that we won the popular vote in 2016 by three million votes while losing the presidential election, there is no way to make this fact go away: losing all those elections in a decade where demographics and issues have been moving decisively in our favor means the Democratic Party has screwed up royally. Even if you write off Hillary Clinton's loss to the Russians, Comey, a bad campaign, her weaknesses as a candidate, 25 years of ugly attacks on her by Republicans, sexism, Bannon's evil racist genius, bad luck, or some toxic stew of those factors, losing all those other elections should make all Democrats fundamentally rethink our political strategy. Democrats are now counting on Trump's unpopularity to solve our problems, but I believe that is a dangerous mistake, because we still haven't solved the foundational troubles that plague us.

Democrats have a boatload of theories on what happened, and what the way forward is, and because of the diversity in ideologies, constituencies, and job descriptions in the Democratic Party, we will never come to a consensus.

People who analyze data and tweak campaign strategies for a living are convinced that we haven't done a good enough job of analyzing and tweaking, and that we would start winning again if we could figure out the right analytic formula.

Some of us believe that the political professionals who run most of the major campaigns and party committees have spent way too much on TV and other traditional ways of communicating to voters, and not nearly enough on social media and new technologies.

People who are focused on voter mobilization of certain constituencies are convinced that we consistently underfund registering voters, turning out the vote, and inspiring their constituencies to vote, and that doing a lot more of those things would turn the tide.

Some Democrats who live in metropolitan areas and have major corporations as clients and/or big contributors think we are getting way too populist in our language and need to "come back to the center." Some Democrats who live in rural states believe we have gotten too caught up in "identity politics" and need to be more focused on the white working class. And many of my colleagues in the progressive populist wing of the party are convinced that if we just had a more populist message and policies, all would be well.

I was a progressive populist before it was cool, and this book will reflect that perspective to a significant extent. But I also am convinced there is no simple formula, no easy panacea for all that ails our party. Maybe my perspective comes from all my years in politics, working in many different kinds of races in different states and regions, including campaigns in a lot of red states. Or maybe it reflects my inherent skepticism of everyone who tries to preach at me that there is only one true way to get things done. I am also acutely aware that if progressive populist messaging and policy was all that it took to elect Democrats, Bernie Sanders would be president, Russ Feingold would be back in the Senate, and Tom Perriello would have been elected governor of Virginia in 2017. Progressive populism can and has worked, but only if we convince voters that in addition to fairness and economic equity, we also care about small business, economic growth, and working people from out in "the sticks" as well as those in the great urban centers on the coasts.

I don't believe there is any one answer to why we screwed up the last ten years. I think we will need to do some mixing and matching of ideas and strategies to create a permanent governing majority for Democrats. However, some of the solutions above are in direct contradiction to each other, and we will need to make choices between them. This book will take a closer look at the strategies being debated and will outline a path that leads to a sustained governing majority for the Democratic Party.

In Chapter 1, I start with a short analysis on what went wrong; discuss what happened in the Obama years; and share where I believe a lot of the blame lies. Doing a deeper analysis of all the things that went awry could make for a historically important and interesting book, although having lived through these years up close and personal, I think it might be too depressing to read without getting addicted to Prozac. This will not be that book, as I want to focus more on solutions for the future than dwelling in the past. However, before we can get to a winning strategy for Democrats going forward, we do need to focus at least briefly on how we pissed our golden opportunity away.

In Chapter 2, I call for an end to the top-down politics of the modern Democratic Party. Currently, many of the major decisions -- which candidates get the party committees' financial support, which consultants and campaign managers run the campaigns, etc. – are made by a small circle of political insiders. This world of big money players and Democratic consultants who at times operate almost as a cartel is powerful, and makes it hard for candidates to do anything but toe the line. Too frequently it leads to a cookie cutter approach to political messaging that hasn't worked well.

The centralized structure of Democratic politics at the national level has led to an arrogance and groupthink that are killing us. That's largely because these political powers are caught up in the conventional wisdom of D.C., which is not in touch with the mood of the country. It's the same folks who thought that Hillary would be the ideal candidate, and that Donald Trump had no chance of winning.

The most frustrating thing about this dynamic was that in 2007 and 2008, Team Obama had brilliantly developed a revolutionary new way of running a presidential campaign. While the management team at the top still had a huge amount of power on some things, they also had, through a combination of social media and traditional field organizing techniques, empowered their local staffers and volunteers to make thousands of day-to-day decisions on how to build the campaign. Unfortunately, the decentralized spirit of that kind of campaign organization faded in the Obama presidency, and by the time of the 2016 campaign, arrogant top-downism was back with a vengeance.

Part of the answer to this dynamic is online activism, fundraising, and political decision-making. A new generation of political leaders are transforming our politics the same way decentralized tech networks changed the American economy late in the last century. Individuals operating out of their homes, with no seed money and no expert advice, have started Facebook pages and online organizations with hundreds of thousands or even millions of followers and can drive more political conversation, trends, and money than some decades-old organizations. We need to listen to these new voices and learn how to incorporate their ideas into our political system. Chapter 3 will analyze the dynamics between top-down and bottom-up politics and sketch out a new paradigm for how the party should reorganize itself.

In that chapter, I begin to sketch out how Democrats can develop a comprehensive strategy. As I said above, we have some real choices to make, as some of the things Democratic strategists (or in some cases pseudo-strategists) argue for are in direct contradiction to each other. But I also make the case that some of the either/or fights about the party are based on assumptions that we shouldn't be making. I strongly believe that old ideas about political alignment are no longer valid (if they ever were), that the "center" described by inside the beltway voices doesn't exist, and that we need to bring fresh thinking to the idea of building a majority coalition.

Part of the bad strategy of the last decade is the old-time conventional wisdom that we must choose between base and swing voters, or between people of color and the white working class. I view these kinds of either/or false choices as foundationally bad - they lead us directly away from victory. Similarly, declaring that we need to choose between fairness and growth in the economy has been proven wrong historically, and sets up a false choice that almost guarantees Republicans a victory in any national election or swing state/district.

I argue in Chapter 3 for Democrats building an agenda and strategy that rejects false choices and embraces multiple good and important things at the same time.

My next two chapters are about the Democratic Party's relationship to constituencies that are currently seen by both the purveyors of conventional wisdom and by some Democrats as at odds with the party.

In Chapter 4, I talk about small-town values and the realities of rural America, which Democrats have been increasingly ignoring over the last decade. This neglect culminated with the 2016 Clinton campaign, when they decided to ignore small-town and rural voters because, according to one campaign aide, "it was just too hard" to reach out to voters there. But Democrats cannot build a governing majority without making inroads into rural America. Simply put, the House, Senate, and Electoral College are all weighted substantially to favor rural areas, and we are not going to change that anytime soon. Besides, Democrats actually have a great deal in common with rural folks both in terms of issues and values, and most people in rural America are poor and working-class people whom progressives ought to be championing.

In Chapter 5, I talk about Democrats' wrong choice, since the Bill Clinton presidency, to work mostly with the biggest businesses instead of cultivating small business and start-up entrepreneurs that could be the heart of a revitalized middle-class-expanding economy. This change of course will take some courage. We have to be willing to take on many of the biggest businesses in the country, enforce anti-trust law, and keep big corporations from getting sweetheart deals from the government.

What progressives and Democrats need to understand is that without small businesses and entrepreneurs, there is no one left to compete with the biggest monopolistic corporations in America.

Unless we want to live in an economy dominated by a few massive conglomerates with overwhelming economic and political power, we need some up-and-comers to start providing competition to the big dogs -- and it's our moral imperative to help them do it.

In Chapter 6, I start by focusing on the strengths and weaknesses of "The Resistance" to President Trump. From the Women's March the day after the Inauguration to the airport protests over the Muslim ban to the student walk-outs protesting for gun reforms after the massacre at Marjory Stoneman Douglas High School, I've been so inspired to watch Americans from all walks of life become engaged in activism against the conservative policies of Donald Trump and the GOP. It's also heartening to see the surge in turnout of Democratic voters in the 2017 elections in places like Virginia and Alabama.

But what does being the opposite of Trump mean? Resistance isn't enough. We need to forge our own agenda as a political party, an agenda that starts with cleaning out the corruption in the system -- the corruption from the Trump years, yes, but also the corruption that permeates our whole political system. I don't believe that we can win elections in any kind of sustained way unless we better define ourselves as a party and tell a story about who we are, what we believe in and care about, and what we will do for the American people. In Chapter 6, I discuss what our agenda as the Democratic Party should be in the years to come.

In Chapter 7, I make a fundamental distinction between how Republicans define freedom and how Democrats should define it. The concept of freedom is at the heart of Americans' belief in their country, and Democrats must start to speak to that belief viscerally. Unlike Republicans, who can't stop talking about freedom, Democrats rarely even use the word or draw a distinction between the parties as to what they mean by it. Ideas matter in the political debate, and we need to put our definition of freedom at the core of how we talk about the Democratic Party. This debate over the definition of freedom -- where Republicans define it as the freedom to do whatever they want no matter whom it hurts, and Democrats define it as the freedom for people to build a better life for themselves and their families -- is at the core of our country's entire political debate.

In my final chapter, I talk about returning to our historical beginnings as the party of the people, the champions of democracy and equality. I'm not being hyperbolic when I say that the Democratic Party started as a radical notion: we were founded in the 1790s as the party in favor of more people having voting and economic rights, and against the big money bankers whom Alexander Hamilton favored. From those days on, Democrats were known as the party of the people. That reputation has eroded in recent years, as more and more people have come to see us as the party of big city and big money coastal elites. We need to get back to our roots.

I want to close my introduction by making clear the fundamental assumption on which I base this book's argument. It is the heart of my aim in writing this book. My assumption is this:

Our goal needs to be a substantial, enduring, decades-long electoral majority. America's next era needs to be the kind of Big Change Moment and electoral realignment that the New Deal was in American history. To get that done, we need to start winning about 55% of the vote.

Since the late 1960s, when the modern course of our politics was put into place, our parties have gone back and forth in power, and our politics has veered from one dead end to another. The result has been a long-term trend of our economy stagnating or declining for most American workers, while the top 1% reaps all the benefits both economically and politically. As a consequence, voters became more and more cynical about both the major political parties, and more and more convinced that our politics and government are broken and corrupt.

Fifty years of politics catering to the plutocracy have brought us to this moment of crisis: our country is being run by an insane, narcissistic grifter with an affinity for totalitarianism, and a Republican Congress unwilling to check his power. People voted for Trump out of a desperation for anyone who might break up the status quo in Washington.

If American democracy is to survive and flourish again, Democrats must resolve to pursue a strategy that isn't just about winning the next election, but instead is about winning governing majorities for a generation -- and then engaging those majorities to make the kind of historically important big changes this country needs to get back on track.

The way we do that is to end top-down politics and empower our grassroots; to break free of either/or politics; to broaden and deepen our coalition; and to lift up America's working families, who have gotten the short end of the stick consistently for the last half-century. Bottom line, we must put the 'democracy' back in the 'Democratic' Party.

CHAPTER ONE: HOW WE GOT OURSELVES TO MESSED UP

Dissecting why we blew our historic opportunity a decade ago isn't the main purpose of this book. Figuring out how we get out of the hole we dug for ourselves is. But before we can get to how we can start winning again and building a long-term governing majority, we need to understand the fundamental causes at the root of our recent failures.

I'll start by saying what it wasn't. The problem wasn't that Obama's presidency failed and he became historically unpopular, as could be said for Jimmy Carter and both George Bushes. Obama had a 55% approval rating going into the 2016 election, and since Trump was elected, his popularity has gone up even more.

The problem wasn't that our issue positioning turned unpopular since 2008. As I indicated in the introduction, a very strong majority of Americans still agree – in some cases, even more so than they did a decade ago – with the Democrats on a wide range of major issues. And it wasn't that any of our core constituencies turned against us. The big base Democratic groups of African-Americans, Latinos, unmarried women, millennials, and urban liberals are all still firmly in the Democratic camp.

The heart of our party's electoral failures is our failure to relate to and deliver for the working class. Note that I did not say white working class: our numbers have been eroding with working-class voters of all races, regions, and sexes. I said above that people of color, unmarried women, and millennial voters are still firmly in our camp, and that is true. But compared to the voting percentages and the voter turnout that we were getting at our high points in 2006 and 2008, we have been sliding with those base demographic groups, as well as white working-class voters.

There are no easy answers for our defeat in 2016; the reasons for our problems are complicated as hell. There is no way, for example, African-American voters were ever going to turn out as well for Hillary Clinton, or any other white candidate, as they did for Obama. There is also no way around the deep cynicism that most non-voters have about politics and politicians in general. But success is also not that far away if we work through the answers to these problems: if Hillary had gotten a higher percentage of base voters to turn out, or if she had gotten Obama's percentage with rural voters, or if fewer progressives had voted for third party candidates as a protest vote, she would have won the presidency. Note that I bolded the or's in that last sentence: any one of those changes would have won her the presidency. However, just one change or another wouldn't have brought us to the 55% we need to create a governing majority, and it wouldn't have been enough for us to win the House back. We need to go far deeper to get that done, but at least Hillary would have been president if any of those things had been different.

Stan Greenberg wrote a thoughtful and important article for The American Prospect where he analyzed this issue. I don't agree with all of Stan's conclusions, but I was especially struck by these critically important ideas:

> Working-class Americans pulled back from Democrats in this last period of Democratic governance because of President Obama's insistence on heralding economic progress and the bailout of the irresponsible elites, while ordinary people's incomes crashed and they continued to struggle financially...

> ...incomes for most Americans fell during this period and the top 1 percent took all of the income gains of the recovery—a subject that mainstream Democrats barely mentioned and did not fight to address...

> ...Closely bound up with the "progress" narrative was the bailout of the Wall Street banks with taxpayer money. Wall Street excess took the country's economy off a cliff and

Democrats rightly came to the nation's rescue by passing the Troubled Asset Relief Program. But the bailout of the banks was, and remains, a searing event in American consciousness—and one inextricably linked to Democratic governance. While the bailout came at the urging of President Bush and his Treasury secretary, it was embraced by then-candidate Obama and passed with Democratic votes in the House and Senate. It was under President Obama that the government signed off on the executive bonuses for TARP recipients and under Obama that no executive was punished for criminal malfeasance. It should come as no surprise, then, that one year after the Housing and Economic Recovery Act's passage, the majority of voters thought the big banks, not the middle class, were the main beneficiaries—and they were damn angry about it too.

One of the most striking statistics I have ever seen in my four decades of poring over exit poll numbers is the following one that I believe sadly sums up the 2010 debacle that began the Democratic Party's devastating decade. In that election, the exit polls asked this question, "Who do you think is most responsible for the bad state of the economy?" The three choices given were Barack Obama, George W. Bush, and Wall Street. Twenty-four percent of the public, basically the most partisan of Democrats, said it was Bush's fault. A very similar but slightly higher number (29%), mostly from the ranks of the most partisan Republicans, said it was Obama's fault. And 35% said it was Wall Street's fault.

The voters who blamed Wall Street were the most populist. They were less partisan in orientation and the most likely to be swing voters. They came heavily from the ranks of working-class voters, and those who had described themselves as independents and moderate. This group voted for Republicans in the 2010 elections by about two to one.

When Obama was running against Mitt Romney of Bain Capital and the 47% tape in 2012, he got more than enough of those voters back. When Elizabeth Warren defeated a popular senator with a moderate image to become the only challenger to beat an incumbent that year, and when Sherrod Brown fought off more money spent against him than any other senator that year to become the only statewide Democrat to win in Ohio since 2006, they won those kinds of voters as well. But as a party, we have gotten our asses kicked with those voters most of the time since our 2008 peak. They became very cynical when Wall Street executives not only didn't go to jail, but got sweet bonuses in the years after crashing the economy. And as Stan pointed out, when the millionaires and CEOs seemed to get most or all the gains from the economic recovery, while working people stagnated, the cynicism grew into a deeper anger.

The Divide Between the Progressive Movement and the Democratic Party Establishment

Working-class swing voters weren't the only ones who got alienated in those first two years of the Obama presidency. When "Too-Big-to-Fail" banks got even bigger and were making money hand over fist in the couple of years after the crash, and the top 1% raked in bigger and bigger money every year, progressives noticed and weren't happy. When Obama looked like he was caving to Wall Street in the early years of the Great Recession, a generation of progressive activists grew more cynical about the Democratic Party and politics in general. The nerve touched by the Occupy Wall Street movement, whose rhetoric at times was as anti-Obama as anti-Wall Street, left a deep impression on thousands of up-and-coming progressive movement organizers and leaders.

Wall Street wasn't the only issue on which populist progressives lost faith with Obama and party leaders. The politics of the health care reform debate was a disaster both for swing voters and for much of the progressive activist community. Progressives had been pushing hard for a single-payer health care system similar to the one in Canada. But when their analysis of Congressional dynamics showed that a single-payer bill had no chance, many progressive organizations and opinion leaders became willing to compromise on a policy idea coined by Yale professor Jacob Hacker called the "public option": the idea that there would be a government-run insurance option for people dissatisfied with private insurance. Given how little competition there was in the private health insurance industry, and how expensive private insurance had become, giving the industry a little competition seemed only fair. Obama, Nancy Pelosi, Harry Reid, and other Democratic leaders publicly embraced the idea, but too many Democrats in Congress were too close to the health care industry, and the public option got left out of the final bill. So did other cost control measures like the government negotiating drug prices and hospitals being forced to go along with cost saving practices.

In the end, after a long, drawn out process that took well over a year and frustrated everyone, a health care reform bill was finally passed. It did do some incredibly important things to improve health care in this country. Far more people were able to get health care coverage, and the insurance industry was no longer able to deny people with pre-existing conditions, as well as older people and women, health coverage and services. Insurance companies even had to use most of their revenue to provide health services for their clients, rather than padding their profits.

But progressives had lost many of the things they had cared the most about in the bill, and were left with a deep sense of disappointment. I kidded my friends in the Obama White House that it was a unique talent to have passed a health care bill that covered far more people than ever before and still left progressives frustrated and angry.

Meanwhile, all that energy and time spent passing health care reform and saving (but not fundamentally restructuring) Wall Street meant that the progressive movement was disappointed in another very big way. High priority legislation that would have reformed the immigration and criminal justice systems, addressed climate change, raised wages and helped unions organize, provided public financing for congressional campaigns, and done several other things that progressives had passionately wanted for a long time got stalled without bills even being brought to the floor for a vote. (There was a very complicated and compromised climate bill that narrowly won a House floor vote, but didn't get voted on in the Senate). And don't forget - this was with the biggest Democratic majorities in both houses of Congress in 30 years.

President Obama deserved a lot of credit for stabilizing the economy after the financial panic of 2008; finally passing a comprehensive health care plan after a century of other presidents trying and failing; and getting a modest, but still important, Wall Street reform bill passed. But he didn't get very much credit from either progressives or populist, working-class swing voters. This was partly because he messed up the politics of it by continually telling everyone how great the economy was doing, even though most voters weren't feeling that way; partly because he failed to achieve big structural reforms that would have taken on and helped tame the entrenched special interests in Wall Street and the health care industry in the policies he did pursue; and partly because he didn't prioritize critical reforms on issues that mattered deeply to the Democratic base.

Most fundamentally, Democratic base voters – just like working-class swing voters – didn't immediately see the kind of tangible improvements in their daily lives that earlier generations of voters saw in the Big Change Moments in American history. Voters in the 1930s saw a steadily improving economy, the money they put in banks insured, a new minimum wage, stronger unions, and retirement income through Social Security. Voters in the 1960s saw the improvements of Medicare and Medicaid, African-Americans saw Jim Crow ending and fair housing laws put into place, and lower income folks saw important improvements in their lives due to the war on poverty. In contrast, voters in 2010 saw jobs still scarce, wages still flat or falling, and Wall Street executives who had caused the meltdown getting the best bonuses they had ever gotten. The Affordable Care Act would improve many people's lives, but it didn't get phased in until 2014, so those improvements weren't noticeable for quite a while.

Democrats should never forget that most of our base voters -- people of color, unmarried women, millennials -- are also working-class. Conventional wisdom punditry puts the Democratic base into a vastly different category than the working class, but economically they look much the same. There are important differences for sure, but lots of similarities. They both were hit very hard by the great recession, as millions of jobs and homes were lost. Over the last decade, they both have seen their wages stay flat while health care costs and other expenses have skyrocketed. Millennials of all races saw big increases in their student debt, while their parents' main source of wealth, their homes, plummeted in value and/or went through foreclosure. Meanwhile rental prices for non-home owners have increased dramatically in recent years due to gentrification, Airbnb rentals, and a variety of other factors. And all throughout this last decade, trying to land a good job with a decent wage and benefits has remained tough.

The fact is that on economics, Democratic base voters look a whole lot like the white working-class voters that everyone keeps talking about, and that fact should be embedded in the brain of every Democrat. Instead, we have fallen into the conventional wisdom of seeing them as too different from each other to have a common agenda, and it has cost us dearly. Here's what Democrats need to know: both groups have been getting screwed, and both are pissed. Their views are identical on a wide range of important issues, and a common agenda which fights for and delivers on those issues would go a long way toward curing our ills.

A focus on universal economic issues won't solve all our problems, though, not by any means. Problems of structural racism go deep and need sustained attention. Democrats need to also understand that issues like immigration and criminal justice reform are central to people of color, and we should never fool ourselves into believing that just talking economics alone will motivate more people of color to vote. We must make solving these problems a central part of our agenda.

The Losses that Have Piled Up

On top of the Democrats in Congress and the White House failing them on the key issues mentioned above, progressives have become politically alienated from the Democratic establishment in D.C. for one more major reason: all those electoral losses that have piled up. Progressive activists and organizations watched as the Democratic establishment pursued strategies that they thought were outmoded -- the old "appeal to upscale white folks in the suburbs with TV ads and cautious candidates" thing -- and continue to lose to Tea Party and Trump-style candidates who weren't trying to appeal to moderates at all.

I have been involved in presidential politics since the 1984 cycle, from D.C. since 1992, and I can point to a completely unsurprising pattern on this subject: when Democrats suffer big losses, the grassroots of the party suffer a lot of angst. Issue, ideological, and message strategy debates go on continually between local Democratic and progressive activists and the national party. But winning elections helps soften the pain of those disagreements. When the national party leaders say "trust us, this is what we need to do to win," and then they do win, those local

7

activists are willing to put up with a lot more. But when we get our asses kicked, the local activists aren't so trusting of the wise party leaders in D.C. The locals start being cheeky enough to think that their ideas on issues, message, and strategy are in fact just as good -- or better -- than the national folks. And so those activists start pushing harder, getting more aggressive. If national party leaders react defensively to this aggressive pushing -- which all too often they have -- it makes matters much worse.

What we have seen over the last decade has been the perfect storm. The economy stayed flat and people didn't see big benefits improving their lives; Wall Street banks kept getting bigger and bankers kept getting bonuses instead of jail time; a health care bill got passed, but no one was seeing immediate benefits; the ugly process and compromises of passing the ACA and Dodd Frank left a bad taste in progressives' mouths; and no action was taken on most of the major issues that the Democratic base is passionate about. With lower Democratic base turnout, populist swing voters mad at Obama's kid gloves treatment of Wall Street executives, and an energized Republican base, Democrats lost the 2010 elections badly. All of this put Democratic activists in a very cynical mood about the national party.

The successful 2012 Obama re-election campaign, combined with some other key victories -- especially progressive icon Elizabeth Warren's Senate victory -- buoyed Democrats' spirits somewhat. But re-districting kept our down-ballot gains to a minimum, and most legislative bodies and governorships remained in GOP hands. When Democrats got blown out again in 2014, the spirits of folks at the grassroots level got doused again.

Going into the Hillary/Bernie battle in 2015, the divide that had opened between D.C. Democrats and local outsider activists in the 2010 cycle was wide and deep, a major reason that this became the most bitter Democratic presidential primary since 1968. The primary was the ultimate proxy war of the insider establishment versus the outsiders and progressives cynical about the party. And when the Russians hacked emails and put their propaganda operation in place to stir the pot, that already bitter schism became an ongoing war that did major harm to Democratic chances in 2016, and has had serious repercussions ever since.

Although this kind of statistic is not easily gleaned from exit polls and other post-election analyses, the best estimates I have seen based on pre-election polling combined with the actual results suggest about 25% of Bernie voters did not support Clinton in the general election. Some, probably around 12%, were so alienated that they went to Trump; a considerable number, much more than in 2012, went to third party candidates as protest votes; and a lot, especially Bernie's younger base, simply didn't show up at the polls at all in November. Those lost Bernie voters absolutely made the difference in Michigan and Wisconsin, where Bernie had won the primaries and the margins were razor thin, and probably cost us Pennsylvania, Florida, and North Carolina as well.

Part of what happened with those Bernie voters who never came around to support Hillary was the brilliantly executed Russian cyber-propaganda operation, and part of it, as I kept complaining from inside the DNC in the last two months of the campaign, was that Hillary's campaign was far too focused in their messaging on upscale suburbanites and not nearly enough at winning back Bernie voters. (We had a better chance at doing the latter with a populist economic message, but the folks in the Brooklyn campaign HQ wanted those upscale suburbanites.) But it was the decade-long ever-deepening divide between grassroots progressives and the Democratic establishment that I described above that was the root cause. Without progressives feeling alienated on Wall Street, health care, and the issues never addressed in 2009-10, without the cynicism that came from those policy decisions and the political strategy decisions that resulted in 2010's and 2014's stunning blowout losses, the seeds that blossomed into the fervor for Bernie in 2015 would never have been planted. And the anger and bitterness over his defeat would never have been so deep and with such consequential results.

Overcoming the Failures of the Last Decade

When Democrats alienated huge swaths of both swing voters and their base, losing elections suddenly became a whole lot more possible, in spite of the demographic and issue advantages we had going into 2009. Democrats created their own perfect storm of devastation in 2010, and doubled and tripled down on it in 2014 and 2016. The end result was that Mitch McConnell would become the Senate Majority Leader, Paul Ryan the Speaker of the House, and Donald Trump the leader of the free world. We will be feeling the consequences of the resulting policy and court decisions for years to come.

The good news is that, as I touched on in my introduction, many of the bleakest moments in American history have been immediately followed by Big Change Moments ushering in our most progressive eras. The darkest-before-the-dawn pattern is a recurrent theme of American history. The decade which saw the passage of the Fugitive Slave Act, the Kansas-Nebraska Act, and the Dred Scott decision, three of the most dreadful, slavery-promoting actions our government had ever taken, came just before the abolition of slavery, the adoption of three profoundly progressive amendments to the U.S. Constitution (the 13th, 14th, and 15th amendments), and the founding of the land grant university system. The Robber Baron era and the height of Social Darwinism in the 1880s and 1890s immediately preceded the Progressive Era, which ended child labor; created the National Park System; advanced food and consumer safety; and resulted in the right to vote for women. The 1920s, which brought the crushing of unions and rampant corruption and speculation in an unchecked stock market, were followed directly by FDR's New Deal and economic reforms that created 40 years of economic stability and prosperity for the largest middle class in the history of the world. (Its great flaw was that it ignored the deep and abiding structural racism in the country's economy, and therefore did not benefit people of color nearly as much as white people). A decade of McCarthyism and rising anti-civil rights violence in the South was soon followed by the breakthroughs of the Civil Rights Movement and the passage of Medicare and Medicaid in the mid-1960s.

So as our country wallows in the worst of the worst destructiveness of the Trump presidency, I can see the potential of another great progressive era in our history. First, though, we need to figure out how to bring those anti-Wall Street populists who voted for Republicans in 2010, 2014, and 2016 into the same tent with the people of color who are being demonized every day by Trump and his allies, and with the progressive base that got so alienated in the lead-up to the Bernie/Hillary showdown in 2016.

If we understand that all three of those groups are made up mostly of working-class folks who have been squeezed by an economic system that has not done well by them for decades, and combine that with a strategy that addresses issues related to racism, we have the potential for getting them to turn out and vote Democratic again in big numbers. And then, if we actually deliver the goods for them and make their lives tangibly, significantly better after we win, we can build a long-term majority coalition that will stretch for years to come.

In New York City, for example, Bill de Blasio won a surprising victory on a strongly progressive populist platform. He has gotten a lot of pushback on his policies from wealthy New Yorkers and a cynical media, but his ability to deliver on his promises, like universal pre-Kindergarten education, meant that he cruised to an easy re-election four years later.

In California, where Democrats hold majority control, they passed legislation to raise the minimum wage to $15 an hour by 2022 and to transition to 100% renewable energy by 2045. Though conservatives like to mock the Golden State as an example of liberal, big government gone wild, Governor Jerry Brown has led the state to a multi-billion dollar budget surplus this year. And according to the New York Times, "California has accounted for about 20 percent of the nation's economic growth since 2010, significantly more than its share of the population or overall output." Apparently higher taxes aren't so economy-dragging after all. Meanwhile, after passing all these progressive laws, Democrats keep getting more popular.

Lest you think that progressive Democrats only govern on the coasts, let me give you one last example from a deep-red state – my friend Nan Whaley, the mayor of Dayton, Ohio. Under her leadership, the city's unemployment rate was cut in half and its economy grew by $600 million. Nan declared a state of emergency over the opioid crisis in her city, and took on the Big Pharma pill pushers, with a lawsuit in 2017. Nan first won office in 2013; the second time she ran unopposed.

Democratic governance, though, must spread and flourish inland. There can be no "flyover country." The alternative -- the kind of political failure that lets people like Trump, McConnell, and Ryan dismantle our democracy and our middle class piece by piece - is unacceptable.

CHAPTER TWO: THE END OF TOP-DOWN POLITICS

One of the main reasons Democrats have been failing to win elections is that our strategies and institutions remain too centralized as the world is becoming more networked and decentralized. The most infamous recent example is the 2016 Clinton campaign's overreliance on its elegant, intricate voter models. The Clinton team worshipped this modeling so profoundly that when field reports from targeted states started flooding in suggesting there was something flawed with the modeling, the local folks knocking on doors and actually talking to people were ignored. It's painful to anyone who loves field organizing and grassroots politics as much as I do to see a small group of data "experts" making all the decisions regardless of what the people on the ground are saying, but that culture reflects a much deeper problem.

After the 2016 election was over, Donnie Fowler, in a brilliant memo he wrote on Medium, had this to say about that culture, and he was right:

> **Top Down, Not Bottom Up: Voters Don't Live in a Voter Model or in DC and Brooklyn.** One key reason that Clinton did not find the same success in 2016 that Obama found in 2008 and 2012 was a different philosophical and strategic approach. The Clinton campaign had a top-down, command-and-control, don't-move-unless-we-give-you-permission culture. It was the polar opposite of the Obama and Silicon

Valley model of top-down leadership and empowerment that is combined with bottom-up collaboration.

After 2008, one of the senior Obama staff, national field director Jon Carson, described their efforts this way: "There's a difference between organizing a campaign & marketing a campaign. We trained & empowered organizers, not volunteers. Carpenters, not tools." This seemed largely lost on the Brooklyn team in 2016.

Instead of combining the human art and hard science of politics, HFA purportedly relied almost exclusively on "objective" polls, voter modeling, and the views of those whose lives and careers are in Brooklyn and Washington, DC.

HFA might have gotten good results in the data lab, but the fact that they didn't show up in the real world means something about the model was flawed. The real question for a post-mortem is not the voter scoring RESULT but (a) whether the INPUTS were correct and (b) whether the reliance on the science of data analytics overly excluded the art of human politics in 2016. No one knows or wants to share (a) and the answer for (b) is apparently "yes, absolutely."

There are two different aspects of the Democratic Party's problem of being too top-down and centralized: its reliance on a consultant cartel and "experts," and its concentration of power within party committees.

When TV Was King

This first aspect involves what I call 'top-down tactics.' Our party's insiders tend to be people like me who cut their political teeth when broadcast TV was king. Back in the 1970s and '80s, we persuaded voters mainly by buying ads -- broadcast TV, cable TV, radio, and newspaper, but mostly broadcast TV, and maybe some direct mail. When your perception is that ads and mail are all that matters, you make all the campaign decisions and execute the vast majority of your budget in a top-down way with just a few people in the room.

Even when TV was king, our campaigns usually spent too much money on it. I have always been convinced that our campaign budgets should allocate more resources to field work -- registering voters, knocking on doors, organizing phone banks, doing absentee and early voting programs, and giving rides to the polls. When we did budget money for ads in the pre-digital days, I have always thought we should spend more on cable TV and radio, and less on the broadcast TV shows that have been shedding viewers since the 1980s. I have been one of the few consultants (along with my fellow consultant Will Robinson, who deserves a shout-out here) who has advocated for this approach.

The advantage of broadcast TV is that it reaches bigger numbers of viewers, or at least used to before those freaky series of internet tubes (as Senator Ted Stevens famously called them) were built and started taking over. The reason consultants like TV so much is that it is a relatively easy and highly lucrative business model: make a few 30 second ads, place the ads on a few shows and then get a commission, historically 15% of the ad buy. In many campaigns today this rate is negotiated lower because of the volume of ads bought, but the take-home pay of the consultant is still pretty hefty.

However much the TV consultants love that business model, the times they are a-changing. Campaigns and consultants are starting to make the transition, but it's not happening nearly fast enough on the Democratic side of the aisle. Republicans have been shifting their dollars to digital far more aggressively.

Friend-to-Friend Organizing

This isn't just a matter of eyeballs, or where we should reallocate ad dollars. After three generations of watching more and more political ads, many of which sound and look almost exactly alike, voters have rightly become more and more cynical of them. In the Trump era, where everything anyone disagrees with is called 'fake news,' and Russian bots and other manipulations of the truth are an everyday occurrence, people are trusting both paid political messaging and traditional news sources less and less. What they do still trust is information from their friends and other known sources, such as organizations they belong to or otherwise respect. Democrats don't just need to shift their ad budgets from TV to digital: they need to shift their tactics toward engagement and organizing rather than just buying ads.

What Democrats need to invest in is decentralized networks of individuals who influence others, and groups that are good at organizing at the national and local level. We need to search for people who are respected by their friends and neighbors, recruit them to be part of our organizing network, and then stay in close touch. If we do this, we can build out a network of networks, and help get those local folks the information and content they need to reach the people they know.

This kind of organizing might be done through Facebook, Twitter, Snapchat or Google groups. It might be done by old school people-to-people activities like door-knocking or house parties or community meetings. While it might seem old-fashioned, with the cynicism and distrust of advertising and even the daily news, decentralized organizing is by far the most effective tool we have. The good news is that with modern technology, we have more ability to mobilize people than ever before. But it still comes down to person-to-person contact. This kind of work isn't so lucrative for consultants in D.C., but it's a better investment than spending ever more money on TV ads.

Here's one example from 2016: my friend Billy Wimsatt took the lead on organizing a group of progressive donors with the idea of moving national money into community-based progressive groups around the country. His organization, called Movement 2016 in that cycle, now called Movement Voter Project, put money into local groups doing people-to-people organizing and voter mobilization on the ground.

In New Hampshire -- where we narrowly won in the presidential race, the U.S. Senate race, and both House races -- Movement 2016 raised $180,000, ran GOTV operations on seven campuses, and recruited 150 full-time, out-of-state volunteers for the final weeks of the campaign. In Nevada -- where we won close victories in the presidential, U.S. Senate, and two competitive U.S. House races, as well as state Senate races that gave Democrats control of the chamber -- they invested $187,000 into nine local groups that did on-the-ground voter registration and GOTV. In North Carolina, where we won a close governor's race in an upset, they raised $300,000 for local groups and organized on 17 campuses. These investments were critical in winning these races, all of which were incredibly close. This is exactly the kind of local institution building and organizing Democrats and progressive donors need to be investing in going forward. And think about the investment described here versus the tens of millions of dollars going into TV ads.

"IBM is to D.C. what Cisco is to Indivisible"

My friend Bob Burnett was a founding engineer at Cisco. In the late 1980s, he left a great job managing hundreds of people at IBM, at the time the dominant tech company on the planet, to help found a start-up that had a radical idea: that the era of big, centralized mainframes running everything in computing was coming to a close, and that the future was the decentralized world of personal computers and the internet.

After the 2016 elections and the online launch of dozens of transformative new groups such as Indivisible, Bob compared the changes in politics to the tech transition in the late 1980s and early '90s:

Now, there's been a comparable shift in the political world. The cognoscenti continue to believe that Washington, D.C. is the center of the U.S. political universe; that everything important happens in D.C., whether it's Trump's latest Tweet or Congressional action on healthcare or the organization of the Democratic Party. But out here in the real world, we don't agree because we think the system is broken. At the moment, that's the belief that unites Republicans and Democrats and Independents and disgusted non-voters: the system is broken and D.C. doesn't get it.

IBM is to D.C. what Cisco is to Indivisible. Cisco represented a fundamental shift from orthodoxy. Indivisible represents a similar seismic shift.

It wasn't just Indivisible, of course. After Trump was elected, all kinds of new groups, from the big ones like Indivisible, the Collective PAC, the Women's March, and Swing Left, to hundreds of smaller community-based organizations all over the country, started organizing and agitating against the right-wing agenda of

16

Trump and the Republicans in Congress. Along with older online organizations and Facebook pages like MoveOn, Daily Kos, the Progressive Change Campaign Committee (PCCC), Democracy for America (DFA), Color of Change, Ultraviolet, Presente, Addicting Info, and Occupy Democrats, their members started showing up at town hall meetings in such big numbers that the Republicans largely stopped holding town halls. They made phone calls, signed petitions, showed up at local demonstrations, shared content on Facebook, recruited candidates for public office, and helped those candidates raise money. And on every major issue that our progressive movement has been faced with in this Trump presidency, from the Muslim ban to DACA, from health care to the tax fight, from net neutrality to gun safety, all these groups plus literally millions of activists have answered the call to arms.

In my 40 years in politics, I have never seen this level of activism and passion, not by a long shot. The closest was the 2005 to 2008 explosion of activism against the Iraq War and the Bush agenda in general (which of course coincided with the big Democratic wave elections of 2006 and 2008). The question now is: how will the Democratic Party respond to this new world of decentralized, online-driven progressive movement building? I have my worries, because what it feels like now is that party insiders, like IBM in Bob's analogy, want to keep control. And here's where we come back to the chasm that has developed between grassroots progressives and the party establishment.

The Recent History of Democratic Party and Progressive Movement Relations

A major part of my work over the last few decades has been as a bridge-builder between the party establishment and the progressive movement. I think it is important to reflect on this history as we discuss the current tension between the decentralized progressive uprising and the Democratic leadership.

When I was cutting my teeth in political organizing in Nebraska and Iowa in the 1980s and early '90s, and then moved into national politics through work in presidential campaigns, the progressive movement was for the most part quite weak and balkanized. The labor movement was stronger then, with considerably more members and money than it has today, but that was the exception to the rule, and even its strength was far eroded from its peak in the 1940s and '50s. Most progressive organizations were single-issue or single-constituency groups and rarely even talked to each other. They were highly centralized, and most of them got their membership through direct mail, which was slow and expensive to process. The grassroots wasn't exactly primed to respond at a moment's notice when big news broke. The urgency and passion of the movements of the 1960s had faded.

The Democratic Party in the 1980s wasn't what you'd call fired up and ready to go either. While we retained control of the House in those years because of the smart and tough tactical leadership of Tip O'Neill and Jim Wright, the party nominated weak and uninspiring presidential candidates three times in a row in that decade, and we lacked a compelling story to tell the American people.

Bill Clinton, for all his flaws, was a great storyteller with enormous charisma, and he really shook the party out of its doldrums. We had lost five of the six presidential elections since 1968, but his 1992 victory reversed that course -- Democratic presidential candidates won more votes in six of the last seven elections since then.

Unfortunately, the top-down structures of the legacy organizations, and the way they were siloed into single-issue groups, kept the progressive movement from waking up for a long time.

I led Clinton's political strategy for working with progressive movement organizations in his 1992 campaign and much of his first term in the White House. We built coalitions to work on the budget and economic plan of 1993; the health care fight of 1993-4; the minimum wage increase and Children's Health Insurance Program that Clinton and Teddy Kennedy pushed through the Republican Congress in the middle and late 1990s; and the big government shutdown fights of 1995. The White House and progressive groups did a lot of good work together in those years, but, again, it was a top-down process. I, along with other White House officials, dealt with the leaders of these balkanized groups, and they mostly followed our lead in terms of strategy and tactics. There was very little feeling of "movement" in the progressive movement of the 1990s.

This created a double-edged problem in terms of progressives' relationship with Democratic politicians. On the one hand, the pols never thought there was much impact to the lobbying and grassroots efforts of the groups when they were on the same side -- they were pretty unimpressed with the power of the movement to influence Democrats in Congress who were straying. On the other hand, Dems like Clinton never really felt much pressure themselves when they started to drift toward the center and toward corporate lobbyists. I have always told people: Bill Clinton at the beginning of his presidency intended to do far more progressive things than he ended up doing, but the pressure was always strong coming from the right, never so much coming from the left. As a result, he kept drifting right.

In the late 1990s, following a new era of continued Republican control of Congress (and then the 2000 Bush election), a growing realization of progressive weakness combined with a little thing called the internet started to change things. First with MoveOn.org's explosive new petition campaigns and other online organizing, then with the blogosphere that blossomed in the early 2000s, then with Facebook pages and other kinds of social media activism, a new kind of progressive organizing began to emerge. More organic in nature, more broadly ideological than single-issue in scope, far better at rapid response, far better at pivoting off the big events and emotional moments in society and culture as well as politics, this new era of decentralized activism led to both amazing successes and big new challenges.

This new progressive movement had its first big wave of success in the second term of George W. Bush. The combination of the Iraq war, Bush's attempt to privatize Social Security, and his administration's botched response to Hurricane Katrina in New Orleans allowed an empowered online activism to raise hell, and then raise money for a new wave of progressive candidates running all over the country. DNC Chair Howard Dean emphasized a "50-State Strategy" and encouraged a crop of grassroots candidates to run in red states and districts previously ignored by the party. In the 2006 Democratic wave, we ran competitive races for Congress in places like Idaho, where we won; Wyoming, where we lost by less than a percentage point; and western Nebraska, where we came closer to winning than we had in decades.

Two years later, this insurgent, change-oriented movement helped fuel Barack Obama's upset of Hillary Clinton in the 2008 primary. The Obama campaign brilliantly played into the new style of decentralized activism. They encouraged supporters to create personal MYBO (My Barack Obama) Facebook pages that allowed them to do their own social media organizing on behalf of the campaign, and they created an exciting narrative around grassroots organizing that was built through training sessions for tens of thousands of local volunteers. The Democratic Party would be far stronger today if we had followed the 2008 Obama campaign's lead and emphasized decentralized organizing. Unfortunately, old habits are hard to break.

In the 1992-2008 era, there were plenty of people who didn't like each other, and naturally some tension, but the relationships and interactions between progressives and the party were, from my perspective, for the most part reasonably healthy. Sure, blogs made Democratic politicians nervous, and the rapid-fire pressure of online petitions, could sometimes make them cranky. Grassroots folks, as they always have and always will, bitched about the D.C. insiders. There were definitely some important issue and ideological differences that I don't want to minimize. But as someone who was trying to bridge and manage these tensions, I felt that the dialogue was more constructive than not. When two Democratic wave elections in a row (which arguably has only happened that one time since the 1930s) brought us to a 37-seat majority in the House, a 60-40 margin in the Senate, and an African-American president who had run on a progressive platform, the political results made the problems seem well worth it.

Then the wheels started coming off.

The Current State of Tension Between the Progressive Grassroots and Party Leadership in D.C.

I'm not going to rehash how the divide deepened between grassroots progressive activists around the country and Democratic Party leaders in D.C. It was depressing enough to write about the first time in Chapter 1. But I do want to talk about the current dynamic and discuss ways to resolve it.

The DNC historically only has the power either a sitting Democratic president or other major party players choose to give it. In the Obama years, unfortunately, that was not much, and the formation of Organizing for America (OFA) created a competing interest to the party both politically and financially. Unfortunately, OFA became a sort of a shadow party, and it was a factor in hollowing out the DNC and state Democratic parties over the last several years.

My friend Jane Kleeb is the Chair of the Nebraska Democratic Party. Jane also knows a thing or two about organizing the grassroots – she founded the Bold Alliance, an environmental coalition of ranchers, Native Americans, and progressive activists dedicated to fighting fossil fuel projects like the Keystone XL pipeline in Nebraska. She had this to say in Politico in 2017:

> With all due respect to President Obama, OFA was created as a shadow party because Obama had no faith in state parties. So I hope the OFA role is none. I hope OFA closes their doors and allows the country and state parties to get to the hard work of rebuilding the party at the local and grassroots level. OFA had no faith or confidence in the state parties, so they created a whole separate organization, they took money away and centralized it in D.C. They gave us a great president for eight years, but we lost everywhere else.

The other big party committees -- the Democratic Senatorial Campaign Committee (DSCC), the Democratic Congressional Campaign Committee (DCCC), and the Democratic Governors Association (DGA) have an enormous amount of power. They have all been very successful not only at raising money, but at developing a big pool of wealthy donors and large Political Action Committees (PACs) that tend to follow their lead on individual races. Which candidates get on their favored list matters a great deal.

To get on the committees' favored lists requires three things. First, you must be from a state or district that party committees deem to be competitive and in play. If you are from a strongly Republican-leaning district, you better have a compelling reason that makes them think you can win despite the odds. There will always be some tensions between the party committees and progressive groups and activists (as well as party locals) as to what districts and states are winnable. In my view, the number of states/districts the party committees target is often too narrow, but targeting by party committees and outside groups is a given.

Second, you must prove, early and throughout the campaign, that you are capable of raising a ton of money. A U.S. House race can now cost $2 million dollars or more, so if your first quarterly report doesn't show some serious numbers, you are likely out of luck with party committee decision-makers. Again, there is some inevitable tension about these formulas and decisions, but many progressive leaders understand this general rationale even as they differ with specific decisions.

Third, the party committee staffers need to think candidates are running the right kind of campaigns. They expect to have a great deal of say about issues and messaging, and they have an approved list of consultants they want you to pick from.

And there's the rub: most of the fighting over the last decade has been around this central control dynamic. The party's losing record over the last ten years has convinced grassroots progressives that party leaders don't know what they are doing. And the fact that those same grassroots progressives have built a powerful decentralized movement that generates millions of members, tens of thousands of activists, and hundreds of millions of dollars has made them very skeptical that D.C. party leaders can win elections any better than they can.

I want to pause here to say something important about the party committees. I worked closely with the DNC in my White House years, and went back inside at the end of the 2016 cycle to try to help salvage a bad situation after Debbie Wasserman Schultz left the place in a mess. I played a role for many years in the late 1990s and early 2000s to help the DSCC have a good relationship with the progressive world, and when Tom Vilsack chaired the DGA, I spent a lot of time working with them on governors' races. I have sympathy for party committee staffers -- they have tough jobs that require pragmatism, and they take an enormous amount of shit. They are paid to elect enough people with a D after their name that Democrats control the majority of the levers of power in this country. Period. I get that. I know that if we have a Democratic Speaker, Senate Majority Leader, and Committee Chairs, the far-right having control over policy and the federal budget will end; Trump will have much more of a check on his power; and if we win the White House and Congress in 2020, progressives will have a chance at passing good legislation. I believe party committee staffers need to have some discretion within that job description to share with donors and PACs they work with which candidates they think are the best for getting elected in a particular race. And I know that some states and House districts are too conservative for strong liberals to win except in unusual circumstances.

I know that not all progressive groups and people agree with that philosophy, but a lot of them do. The problem with the system that we have right now is that some party committee staffers and consultants adhere too closely to the D.C. conventional wisdom about what kind of candidates to pick and how to run campaigns. Some of them believe they know best, even if in-district Democrats and the progressive groups doing good work on the ground think they are all wrong. The blunt truth is that some of the consultants on the approved lists for the party committees are long-time D.C. insiders who use stale campaign tactics and make mushy campaign ads. Too many of them still think that the most critical target in most races are high income suburbanites rather than working-class folks of both the base and swing variety, and that self-funders or candidates with ties to corporate donors are always the best kind of candidates.

Party committee staffers too often tend to favor cautious centrists, the "safer" candidates, rather than the grassroots-motivating, bold champions that progressives believe will generate better voter turnout and raise more money online. When the party committee staffers make those kinds of choices, the divide between grassroots progressives and party insiders once again deepens. Especially when those handpicked party committee candidates depress activist and base voter turnout, and then go on to lose their elections to Republican extremists, as happened a lot in the 2014 and 2016 cycles.

This is a dynamic no one in the Democratic Party on either side of the divide should take lightly. We need a united party. We need honest dialogue. The irony is that I had dozens of conversations in the '90s and early 2000s with Bill and Hillary Clinton, Tom Daschle, and other party leaders about the need to build a stronger grassroots progressive movement that could register and turn out more voters, recruit and train more volunteers and young candidates, and raise more money. Those Democratic leaders wanted that kind of grassroots strength back then, and now we have exactly that kind of movement. The grassroots Left is energized and stronger than ever, which is the good news. The tough part for Democratic insiders is that this more robust progressive movement has its own ideas, message, and strategies. Its leaders have their own constituencies to satisfy and their own political positioning choices to make. Party leaders need to make space for these powerful new allies, and be willing to work with them as colleagues and peers.

Bullying vs Bridge-Building

The approach of some Democrats to challenges from the left is to turn into bullies. There are plenty of examples of this at every level of politics, but I can attest to the fact that bullying in politics almost never works, and is generally about the stupidest thing you can do.

Here's one example that came up as I have been writing this book. New York Governor Andrew Cuomo has been irritated by progressives pressuring him from the left for a long time. Cuomo is being challenged in 2018 in a primary by Cynthia Nixon, who is a well-known actress, but also a long-time progressive activist. Cuomo had a meltdown: he told labor unions to drop their support of progressive allies supporting Nixon or that he would never return a call from them again. The supporting groups in question were organizations including Working Families Party, New York Citizen Action, New York Communities for Change, Progressive Action Network, and Make the Road Action. While sadly some of the unions went along with the bullying, none of those progressive groups backed down one inch, and they are redoubling their efforts to elect Nixon. Cuomo's bullying has created a firestorm of bad press. Beyond that, in my judgment, Cuomo's hopes to become president are now dashed. The Iowa and New Hampshire progressives who dominate Democratic politics in those states don't take kindly to bullies, and they will kill his chances quickly, no matter how much money he raises.

On the other hand, if you reach out in the right way, progressives will respond well to Democrats: think about all the support progressive candidates like Elizabeth Warren and Bernie Sanders have received from the progressive community. Even beyond those obvious favorites, I can tell you from my days working for a moderate president, Bill Clinton, that we had a great relationship with the progressive community. My goal as the main liaison with the progressive world was to listen to their views in advance, and brief them on the different options in front of us. If we made a decision they would be unhappy with, I was on the phone with people right before the news broke, giving them the heads up. I explained our thinking and asked what kinds of things we could do for them to soften the blow, so that we could work together on other priority issues in the future. That bridge-building fostered a great deal of loyalty to Clinton, and was the main reason so many groups stayed in his corner during tough times. In retrospect, given some of the decisions later made on issues like Wall Street deregulation (although I was out of the administration by then), I sometimes think I did my work too well: the administration got too little shit for some of the policy decisions that came down the pike.

Closing the Chasm

To start winning elections again, and certainly in order to build effective governing majorities that can deliver for the American people, this chasm between the grassroots movement and Democratic insiders needs to be, if not closed, at least bridged.

My insider friends bitch a lot about how unfair some progressive activists are to them, resenting the notion that all insiders are corporate shills or rich party hacks. And my progressive activist friends bitch a lot about criticism from beltway insiders who say they are unrealistic and naïve.

Both sides are, in my judgment, right some of the time. But to party insiders, hear this: you don't win elections by bitching about how dumb the voters are (as I heard some Democrats doing after the 2016 elections), and you can't build a winning political strategy by complaining about how your grassroots activists are unfair to you. To win, we need a unified party and Democratic insiders must take it upon themselves to genuinely reach out and build bridges.

Here are some humble suggestions on next steps:

1. **Build relationships with the grassroots.** Party committees should do far more outreach to netroots/grassroots groups. I did a lot of this years ago for different party committees -- giving groups a heads up on things that were happening, working to put out the inevitable fires that flare up, and having honest conversations about which candidates are the most likely to win which races. There are always going to be disagreements, but talking things through does make things easier, at least most of the time.

   I give Nancy Pelosi a lot of credit in this regard. She has made it a point to do regular conference calls with grassroots progressive groups and Facebook pages over the last couple of years, and it has improved her relationship and standing with those activists. Other party leaders and committees need to do more of the same.

2. **Spend more time meeting with local progressive activists when you are in-district.** I know party committee leaders and staffers are busy as hell, but they go out on the road all the time to talk to candidates and campaign staff. They should take the time to meet with local allied groups to open up lines of communication as the election cycle goes forward, so that the locals feel like they are heard. A great model for this is what Keith Ellison has been doing in his role as the deputy chair of the DNC. When Keith travels around the country, he almost always makes a point of scheduling a meeting with local progressive groups and activists. These meetings have gone a long way to tamp down the hostility toward the DNC coming out of the ugly divisions of the 2016 cycle.

3. **Be diverse in your hiring decisions.** One of the things Steve Phillips has done terrific work on is pushing for the party committees to do a better job in hiring people

of color as both staffers and consultants. Progress has been slower than it should be, but his efforts have started to bear results, and I know from multiple conversations with party committee leaders that the committees are far more sensitive to hiring people of color as staff and consultants than they used to be.

The same kind of conscious thinking about diversity of political perspectives needs to be employed as well. Groupthink is one of the worst things that can happen in any institution, and particularly in politics. That is especially true when our party is as deeply divided as it is now.

Party committees should go out of their way to hire staffers and consultants who come from the progressive organizational world, the world of online organizing, and the ranks of people who worked for progressive politicians. The DSCC bringing on Mindy Myers, Elizabeth Warren's ex-chief of staff, as executive director for the 2018 cycle was a good step forward, for example. Relationships, biography, and perspective all matter, and in my experience over the last ten years there has been too much drawing from the same pool of people in committee hiring. I would also add that the approved vendor list that the party committees give to campaigns should be diverse in political perspective and history, as well as ethnicity, gender, and sexual orientation. This isn't a matter of "bean counting" or tokenism: diverse perspectives and biographical backgrounds in a diverse party are essential to building a winning strategy.

Changing the culture of party leadership so that it is more embracing of, and more communicative to, the decentralized world of the grassroots progressive movement is going to be challenging. Entrenched cultures and business models are hard to change. But until we do change, the destructive divide between Democratic Party leadership and the progressive world is going to continue to deepen.

Ultimately, what we need is for party leaders to understand the new decentralized world we are living in, and to embrace the people and at least some of the ideas of the grassroots movement that is rapidly building power and taking over the party from the ground up.

We can't build a winning strategy by rejecting our base and dismissing all their ideas and candidates. Whether we like it or not, whether we are comfortable with it or not, the decentralization paradigm is here and the Democratic Party must adapt or die. In the meantime, all those decentralized organizations and activists should keep on changing the world.

CHAPTER THREE: THE 55% GOVERNING MAJORITY

The goal of the Democratic Party must be to build a long-term governing majority that can bring big changes and real improvements to the lives of lower and middle income Americans. Only by achieving that goal do we break the destructive cycle of the last 40 years that has given rise to Trumpism. However, in order to build the kind of coalition that can pull this off -- one that can win the presidency, U.S. Senate, U.S. House, and a majority of gubernatorial seats and state legislative chambers -- we need to do something really big and really important: end the debate over false choices that too many people in our party love to have. For my entire career, many of my progressive friends have argued that all we need to do is turn out the base vote. At the same time, many of my friends in the more establishment side of the party, while giving lip service to the need for GOTV operations, are singularly obsessed with appealing to swing voters, and pour the vast majority of their campaign's budgets into that tactic.

Let me pause to add one key caveat: the whole swing vs. base notion is pretty damn fuzzy to begin with. There are tons of voters in base demographic groups who occasionally vote Republican depending on the year and the candidate, who sometimes consider voting for a third party candidate, and who definitely have to be persuaded that voting actually matters. And there are plenty of "swing" voters who may well decide not to bother to vote at all, which makes them the ultimate variable. A lot of voters are in their own particular categories. For example, voters who tend to vote for one party in national elections, but are much more open on whom they will vote for in local races. Bottom line, there are all kinds of voters, and we need to be careful about making too many sweeping assumptions.

We need to be successful, at least more successful than we have been in the last decade, with both base and swing voters, with rural and small-town folks as well as big city voters, with the "Rising American Electorate" (RAE) and with older, whiter constituencies. (Being successful with different constituencies doesn't mean the same thing with every constituency, of course. We don't need to win a majority in all these groups, just be able to compete more effectively in all of them.) We need to create a party identity, a message, and an issue agenda that can appeal to people in every region, and that can have a real chance at consistently getting 55% or more in a national election.

This isn't wishful thinking; we aren't that far away from winning elections by good margins more consistently. Since 1992, Democrats have received more votes in all but one presidential election, and in four of those seven elections we have won by four points or more. Since 2006, if you add up all the votes in all the races around the country, Democrats have totaled more votes on both the House and the Senate side than Republican candidates every year except 2010 and 2014, and six times -- four times on the Senate side, twice on the House -- have won by margins of over seven points. (Republicans have won more races than these numbers might indicate due to the combination of gerrymandering and the Senate bias toward small states.)

The combined RAE percentage of eligible voters is already over 55%, and growing every year. A black man with an African Muslim name got 53% of the vote in 2008, and in 2012, despite a very tough economy and a lot of big mistakes politically in his first term, he got re-elected with 52%. Even Hillary Clinton, whose campaign was beset with many bad breaks and was far from perfectly run, got three million more votes than Trump. And all the while, the demographic clock ticks steadily in our favor, as our party's base demographic groups grow and base Republican demographic groups shrink.

But even with all those nice statistics, today Republicans control the presidency, Senate, House, and most state governments. Democrats can't win or govern consistently by choosing whether to engage with base or swing voters. We must do both. And the idea that we must make a choice, while I respect the arguments of those who make them, ultimately won't get us where we need to go. Democrats have the resources to message and organize in a wide variety of communities.

We can create an issue platform and message that can appeal to both Democratic base voters in the RAE and working-class swing voters. It won't be easy to get Democrats to move in this direction, for reasons I outline later in this chapter. We have some serious credibility issues with a lot of voters on whether we will ever deliver for them, and whether we even give a damn about them at all. Intense cultural issues must be overcome, including some serious divides within the Left in terms of race, sex, religion, and region.

But the path is there if we choose to take it.

The Argument for Focusing on the Base

My friend Steve Phillips, who has been one of the most influential civil rights activists in the country for many years, wrote a brilliant and compelling book published in early 2016 called Brown Is the New White: How the Demographic Revolution Has Created a New American Majority. Steve's book does a great job laying out the numbers showing the political power of the demographic changes in America. He argues that because of these demographic changes, Democrats already have a clear majority of voters in their camp, if only they would do the work and spend the money to turn them out. Steve also argues that worrying about swing voters is pretty much a waste of time.

This seems to be a direct contradiction to the case I am making, and in some ways, it certainly is. But I was so impressed with Steve's argument, and thought it was so centrally important for the Democratic establishment to hear, that I became a part of Steve's team to help market the book.

I know, I know, you're probably a little confused right now. Before I explain my thinking, let me summarize Steve's central argument.

Backed up with impressive statistics, Steve made the case that the dramatic growth in people of color as a percentage of the

American population, combined with the votes of white people who tend to vote for progressive candidates, is already a majority of the American public. He believes that if the Democratic Party used most of its money to turn out people of color and, to a lesser extent, progressive whites, instead of on TV ads targeting swing voters, Democrats would win consistently and win big. He wrote an op-ed in the New York Times on October 5, 2016:

> In November, Democrats have the chance to secure a decades-long electoral majority for decades, but they are at risk of missing this moment because too many consultants still stick to an outdated and ineffective campaign script that was written for a different, whiter era. Democratic spending is significantly misaligned with the pillars of the party's electoral advantage, and campaigns throw away millions of dollars on ineffective ads while neglecting efforts to mobilize the rapidly growing ranks of minorities.
>
> The evidence about the formula for Democratic victory at the national level is overwhelming. When large numbers of voters — particularly minorities — turn out, Democrats win. When turnout plummets — as it did in midterm elections in 2010 and 2014 — Democrats lose.
>
> But the evidence has not translated to the actual practice of those who run and fund Democratic campaigns...
>
> Another problem: The target audience for ads, swing voters, is dwindling. A 2015 study by a Michigan State University assistant professor, Corwin Smidt, shows that voters are more polarized than at any time in the past 60 years, and just 5 percent — about six million people in the 2012 electorate — are swing voters. By comparison, the number of eligible minority voters in 2012 who didn't make it to the polls was more than 25 million.

Tragically, Steve's words of warning about Democrats missing their moment in 2016 turned out to be true. The turnout of black voters and young voters was weak compared to what it should have been. If we had pushed the levels of turnout even just a little higher among those cohorts, we would have won PA, MI, WI, NC, and FL, prevailing in both the presidential election and the Senate races in PA and WI. And Steve was right about the swing voters that the Clinton campaign targeted with all those TV ads: not nearly enough Republican-leaning women in the suburbs swung to Hillary, despite Trump's odiousness as a person.

Steve's work is primarily focused on the need for Democrats to spend much more of their money and messaging resources on people-of-color engagement and turnout. One of his central arguments is that finding new voters in the demographic groups already aligned with us is more efficient than spending ever-increasing sums chasing elusive and mysterious white swing voters. I think he's more right than wrong, that our spending priorities definitely need revamping, and that a message strategy that is so obsessed with a small number of hard-to-find moderate white voters does in fact dampen the enthusiasm we need among people of color.

Steve also puts his money where his mouth is, raising millions of dollars in recent years for on-the-ground voter mobilization of communities of color. One of his efforts was critical in the Alabama Senate special election in December of 2017. With funds Steve raised, Marvin Randolph (one of my partners) ran a black voter turnout project that was the central force in turning out enough black voters to win that election for Doug Jones. There is not even a glimmer of a question in my mind that if that money had gone into more TV ads instead, we would have lost the election.

I have three observations about Steve's central thesis:

First, on the whole turnout thing: one of the biggest historic mistakes of the Democratic Party's electoral strategy is focusing on communities of color only a couple weeks out from the election. The thinking has usually been that those voters are base voters, so we don't need to talk to them until it is time to turn them out to vote.

This is what leads to cynicism and weak results. The Democratic Party needs to be investing in local leaders, organizers, activists, and community groups in communities of color all year around, not just right before the election. Our party and its candidates need to hear what is going on in these communities, listen to what issues matter the most to them, and make the investments that show we have a stake in their lives and their well-being. We need to recruit, train, and develop young organizers and leaders who will spread the word and get people motivated. If we fail to do this, we will continue to get voter turnout below what we could be and should be getting.

If you want to see a great example of this kind of long-term community building and investment and what it produces in terms of turnout, take a look at the way Congressman Keith Ellison's political operation has yielded higher and higher vote totals for Democratic candidates up and down the ticket in Minneapolis, turnout that has been essential to Democrats winning statewide elections there.

Second, Steve's point about the party needing to have better representation among both our operatives and our candidates is exactly right. In order to understand, engage, and motivate communities of color we need to have people of color involved every step of the way, at all levels of the decision-making structure -- including at the candidate level. At the highest level, Democrats should never have a presidential ticket of two white men ever again. It just doesn't represent our party. And I would argue strongly that at least one of the two should be a person of color.

Third, and where I agree most profoundly with Steve, I think we can't have a strategy that requires us to be mushy about our commitments to immigration, criminal justice reform, and other issues central to people of color. If that means we lose some votes of white people who think immigration is a problem or that cops should never be questioned, so be it. I don't think we will lose many, because I believe most white voters who think that way are already firmly ensconced inside the Republican Party. Steve's numbers are convincing: we can pick up far more votes from people of color if we don't back away from their issues than the white voters we would lose. I will also make the argument later that there are still enough swing, working-class white voters who will accept our stands on racial justice to give us the percentages we need.

Before I leave Steve's book, I think it's important to add a little more detail about the whole rather broad category of "progressive whites," which Steve says is 28% of the electorate. That 28% is a little bit of a funky category, especially given the numbers of voters who (a) voted for Obama and then voted for Trump; or (b) voted for Jill Stein or other third-party candidates as a protest against Hillary.

The good news is that most of that 28% does vote pretty consistently for Democratic candidates and progressive ballot initiatives. These voters are a lot more likely to be women than men and tend to be younger, with both Gen X and millennial whites considerably more likely than baby boomers and older voters to vote Democratic. Unmarried whites, both men and women, but especially women, tend to be much more Democratic than married whites. Whites who are not religious at all, and those who are not traditional Christians -- Jews, Muslims, Buddhists, Hindus, etc. -- tend to lean more Democratic. White union members are much more likely than other white working-class folks to vote for Democrats. Other white progressives include feminists, environmentalists, and most folks in the LGBT community.

Some of these demographic groups have historically had relatively low voter turnout rates, and need a major dose of Get-Out-the-Vote (GOTV) work every election year. Younger people are notoriously tough to turn out; single women are less likely to turn out than their married sisters; people who are not regular churchgoers are less likely than their church-going neighbors to show up at the polls.

Demographics aside, there are plenty of pockets of progressive white voters even in cohorts not as Democratic as the ones listed above. Hillary Clinton did worse than any Democratic presidential candidate since Walter Mondale among rural voters, for example, and she still got about a third of those voters. Bernie Sanders did great in the Democratic primaries in a lot of rural states and counties. I am a straight, married, white, male baby boomer, and I have a lot of friends and family in the same demographic cluster who are liberal Democrats. With the ability to micro-target on a granular level, we should be able to find all of these pockets of progressive folks wherever they are.

Steve is fundamentally right, I would say about 95% right: we do have a progressive voting majority in this country, and if we devote far more of our resources as a party and progressive movement to turning that majority out, we will win a lot of elections. The question is whether it gets us to that enduring governing majority, and I don't believe it currently does for reasons I will explain below.

The Argument for Focusing on the White Working Class, Especially in Rural Areas

Let me start this section by saying that, as I noted above, there are a group of Democratic operatives who think that swing voters are the end-all be-all when it comes to winning Democratic campaigns. Their assumption, as far as I can tell, is that base voters have nowhere else to go, and will be motivated to vote because of how awful the Republicans are on the issues, or maybe just how awful they are personally. This argument on its face is absurd: all you have to do is look at turnout numbers of key demographic groups to know how much turnout among base voting groups varies election to election, or look at research on what works in GOTV programs to know that just trashing your opponent doesn't maximize your turnout numbers. However, there are plenty of smart people (not the Democratic operatives I describe above), who believe strongly in both base turnout and swing voter persuasion, and I will focus on their arguments in this section.

There is no analog for Steve's book that I know of for the opposing argument that Democrats should focus more on swing voters, particularly the white working class, but there are certainly an array of good strategists who have made the case. One of their central points is that the working-class voters we have lost in recent elections are mostly in rural areas and smaller towns, and that those losses point to big problems winning majorities in the electoral college, the Senate, and the House. Some of the people who make this argument are small-state politicians who are naturally biased toward this point of view, but some of them are people with a national perspective.

For example, the legendary student and labor organizer Paul Booth, who tragically passed away in early 2018, was for most of his career one of the top organizers and strategists for AFSCME. Despite his big city roots and labor organizing orientation, Paul was one of the leading advocates of a rural strategy for Democrats. (He and I also shared the belief that devoting massive resources to organizing and GOTV for the base is critical to winning elections.)

Paul once said to me that we don't just need a 50-state strategy: we needed a 3,142-county strategy (the total number of U.S. counties). He believed that to win state legislative chambers, as well as the majority of congressional and statewide races, we couldn't keep getting blown out of the water in rural and small-town America. Paul believed in organizing everywhere.

Another eloquent advocate for Democrats paying more attention to rural areas and small towns is former Iowa Governor and United States Department of Agriculture Secretary Tom Vilsack, another old friend. In his gubernatorial races, Tom did very well for a Democrat in Iowa's rural counties, and with working-class voters in medium-sized cities like Ottumwa and Dubuque. As Obama's Agriculture Secretary, he made major investments in economic development and housing programs in rural America, and traveled the country talking to small-town folks Democrats rarely or barely even try to reach. Tom came away convinced that if we made a serious effort in these areas, Democrats could fare far better. More on Tom's ideas in Chapter Four.

Unfortunately, Hillary's campaign chose not to make this kind of investment. The campaign did have a rural coordinator, and they sent out some surrogates to small towns on occasion, including even the Big Dog (meaning Bill Clinton) himself. But Hillary herself rarely showed up on the campaign trail in smaller towns and counties, and hardly ever talked about issues directly impacting rural America. Booth, Vilsack, and I, along with a lot of other good folks, all made the case strongly to the campaign that we needed to be doing more in the rural countryside. Even Bill Clinton weighed in with the campaign to make this case. But as one Clinton staffer said after the 2016 election, the campaign had decided it was "just too hard" to target rural voters.

The results showed the lack of effort: Hillary only got about a third of rural/small town voters amid a stronger than usual rural turnout. By contrast, 20 years earlier, Hillary's husband – after passing two gun control laws, promoting LGBT rights more than any president had to that point, and vetoing a late term abortion bill – won around 45% of rural/small-town voters. Barack Obama – the big city black guy with the African Muslim name – matched Bill Clinton's 45% among rural/small town voters in 2008, according to exit polls. He slipped some in 2012 after four years of a tough economy, but still got close to 40%.

Democrats like Booth and Vilsack who have argued for a renewed focus on rural/small-town voters point to the electoral math of the American system that disproportionately weights rural voters and small states far more heavily than urban voters. As Emily Badger put it in the New York Times in a November 20, 2016 article:

> Rural America, even as it laments its economic weakness, retains vastly disproportionate electoral strength. Rural voters were able to nudge Donald J. Trump to power despite Hillary Clinton's large margins in cities like New York. In a House of Representatives that structurally disadvantages Democrats because of their tight urban clustering, rural voters helped Republicans hold their cushion. In the Senate, the least populous states are now more overrepresented than ever before. And the growing unity of rural Americans as a voting bloc has converted the rural bias in national politics into a potent Republican advantage.

Just think about the Senate for a moment. If you add up the people who live in Alaska, Delaware, Idaho, Maine, Montana, North and South Dakota, Utah, and Wyoming, their combined population is barely over 11 million, while California has over 39 million residents. Those nine states have 18 senators representing them, while California only has two. Another way to look at it: the population of the 19 states with two Republican senators is a little over 100 million, while the 18 states with two Democratic senators have a combined population of almost 140 million. (Thirteen states have one each.) These numbers make it clear that controlling the majority of seats in the Senate requires a rural working-class strategy.

Rural/small-town, working-class folks are not the only ones we should be targeting, either. Plenty of Americans who are financially pressed and living paycheck to paycheck live in cities and the suburbs, and a lot of them live in state legislative and congressional districts that we need to win control of Congress and state legislative chambers. Some of these voters are older voters, and appeals to them on the basis of Democrats fighting for Social

Security, Medicare, and Medicaid could help us gain more votes from seniors. Some of these folks are union members, who can more easily be reached and persuaded by unions and Democrats. But the labor movement has been declining as a percentage of the workforce for a long time now, which means that Democrats have to work harder at getting their share of these votes.

The Mysterious Well-to-Do Swing Voters in the Suburbs

Another of the big theories in Democratic politics, a theory that has been the animating driver of most of our party's leadership since at least the early 1990s, is that the most important swing voters in American politics are well-to-do white people in the suburbs. Centrist pollster Mark Penn famously called them "soccer moms" and "office park dads." Hillary Clinton devoted way too much of her 2016 campaign's money and messaging firepower to this demographic.

Let me start by highlighting the well-to-do part. There are a huge number of working-class and poor folks of all races living in the suburbs. Those voters should be targeted more than they currently are for persuasion and GOTV. My focus for this section, though, is the upper-income suburbanites, whom I think party leaders have over-emphasized in their political calculations.

These upper-income voters did have some importance to both Clinton's and Obama's presidential victories. They also moved in our direction in 2016, as a lot of them didn't like Trump. Additionally, this bloc of voters particularly matters in some key House districts and Senate races. So I am not an advocate of writing off this demographic group entirely as part of the potential Democratic electoral coalition. I do believe, however, that we are over-obsessed with them. For example, when I look at the way Hillary Clinton's campaign messaging, advertising dollars, and direct mail dollars were focused so heavily on this cohort, and then I look at the voting tallies, I have to shake my head.

The first thing to keep in mind is the raw number of high-income voters. A lot more Americans are working- and middle-class than upper-income. Over 43% of American households have incomes under $50,000 a year, even when you add up multiple people working in the household. Another 29% plus of households bring in between $50,000 and $100,000. Households with incomes over $100,000 are the smallest of the three categories, at less than 28%. And by the way, most of those over $100k households are clustered pretty close to the bottom of that spectrum. Only 7% make over $200,000, for example, and when you and your spouse are each making in the low $50s in an urban area, you don't feel "high income." Also keep in mind that big numbers of those high income folks have as their primary residence a home in big cities instead of the suburbs, lowering the number of well to do suburban voters even more.

Second, upper-income folks are just not as swingy as Democratic insiders think they are. Since my time on the 1992 Clinton campaign's targeting committee, I have closely followed every bit of data I can get from all kinds of sources -- internal campaign and party committee polls, exit polls (although they have been shown to be pretty unreliable in some regards), analysis done by groups like the Analyst Institute and Catalist, the great ongoing polling and analysis work done by Democracy Corps, the regular Battleground polls released by Celinda Lake and The Tarrance Group, and polling reports from a variety of other groups I've worked with. I have never in that quarter century of reviewing polling noticed any trend toward suburbanites with high incomes being any more "swing-y" than any other demographic group.

In fact, my strong sense is that working-class demographic groups tend to be far more volatile than upper-income suburban voters. Small-town and rural voters, people making under $30,000 a year, whites without a college degree -- these categories of voters have moved all over the place from election to election, many times in bigger numbers than high-income suburbanites.

One of the reasons well-to-do voters may well be less swingy than other cohorts is that they tend to be better educated, more informed about candidates' positions on their issues, and more in touch with the political system. Swing voters tend to be less informed, less educated about the issue positions of candidates, and less connected to politics in general. For those high-income, better-educated suburban voters who care a lot about issues like the environment, gun safety, reproductive choice, and LGBT rights, the odds are already pretty good that they are loyal Democrats. High-income voters who prioritize low taxes are probably Republicans. The number of voters who swing wildly from party to party just doesn't tend to be as big.

Finally, the results of the special elections that have played out over the course of the 2018 electoral cycle as of this writing provide more evidence that our obsession with well-to-do suburban voters over blue-collar voters has been ill-founded. Our entire Democratic Party structure invested massive sums in trying to win a well-to-do suburban Atlanta special election race in mid-2017. The candidate, Jon Ossoff, and associated party committees raised and spent an absurd $40 million-plus in that race -- far more than any House race in history -- and ended up losing 52-48. The other three U.S. House specials that year were all in more blue-collar districts in Kansas, Montana, and South Carolina, and the national party spent very little in those races. We lost all three, but although those races were virtually ignored, we came closer to victory in South Carolina than in Georgia, and nearly as close in Montana and Kansas. Meanwhile, in the blue-collar Alabama Senate race last December, the blue-collar House district in Pennsylvania in March of 2018, and in special elections for state legislative seats in blue-collar districts in OK, WI, and NH, we won big upset victories.

The over-focus on upper-income voters comes from several things. One is simply that while party insiders come in many shapes and sizes and include people of color, labor leaders, and old progressive warhorses like me, many party insiders in D.C. are in fact part of this demographic: upper-income whites who live in the suburbs. Their neighbors and friends, the people they talk to most of the time, tend to be the same. When everyone you hang out with tends to think the same way, it's easy to think that is what most people think.

Another reason is that the big donor base for the party, the people party insiders are forced to spend an inordinate amount of time with, are mostly these upper-income, suburban whites. These big donors tend to be liberal on social issues, but using a working-class oriented economic populist message when you are courting them every day can get pretty damn uncomfortable at times. I have been in dozens of strategy discussions in campaigns over the years where the political staff and pollsters were recommending a tough populist message, but the people responsible for raising the money balked at a strategy that would offend the donors.

The third reason party insiders tend to focus on well-to-do suburbanite voters is that for many of them, their future, or even current, clients are well-heeled business people. Many Capitol Hill, White House, and political campaign staffers go on to become lobbyists or PR consultants for business interests, and they have an incentive to make sure their messaging appeals to potential employers. And some consultants simultaneously work for Democratic candidates and business clients, which can make a mushy, cautious economic message more palatable.

Now, there is nothing wrong with making an appeal to well-to-do suburbanites, especially ones we have identified as caring deeply about issues like gun safety, women's rights, and the environment. But the problem with over-emphasizing these voters is that you are likely to de-emphasize an economic message that appeals to, motivates, and unifies the working- and middle-class voters Democrats need to put together a sustainable majority.

I've laid out some ideas on why we need to emphasize our appeal both to the Democrats' base and to swing voters, but as I have said above, doing both simultaneously isn't a simple or easy thing to pull off. There are at least two big barriers we are going to have to overcome. The first one is of the progressive movement's own making.

A Big Challenge: Political Correctness

An enormous challenge for Democrats and the progressive movement in terms of appealing to working-class voters is our own political correctness. Trump's ranting against political correctness has consistently been one of the very best things he has going for him politically. In every working/middle class focus group I have seen over the last two years, even when people dislike almost everything Trump does, people talk about how much they like his lack of political correctness. Even when he steps over the line and offends people, he can always fall back on "hey, sorry I offended some people, I'm just not politically correct" and survive.

We know that when Trump does the political correctness stuff, he wants to justify his own racism, sexism, xenophobia, etc. But there's a reason it resonates, and that is because to regular folks, having the way you've communicated all your life (and you in extension) picked apart and condemned is hard to take.

Quick story about my early days as an organizer. I had a mentor from the Machinist Union named Bill Fenton. Bill was one of the greatest organizers I have ever known, and was one of Iowa's leaders in fighting for progressive policies of all kinds. He was especially passionate on civil rights issues. I'd heard him give many a stemwinder on the topic at Democratic Party conventions. One day in the bar, one of his fellow Machinists started to tell a racist joke. I was outraged, was about to cut the guy off, but Bill signaled me to let him continue. After he was done, Bill laughed and said, "That was a funny joke, Eddie. But you know our union brother Jim down at the plant? What would he think about that joke?" (Jim was clearly an African-American man.) Eddie's face turned red with embarrassment and he told Bill, "I would never tell that joke in front of Jim." Bill said, "Well, that's good, because he'd probably punch you. But you should think about him and our other black union brothers and sisters when you tell jokes like that. We need them when we are fighting the boss, and Jim and the other black folks at your plant always stood with us."

Bill was gentle with Eddie throughout the conversation. He didn't get on his moral high horse, and he didn't talk down to him. But by the end of the conversation, Eddie promised Bill he would never tell a joke like that again. It was a good lesson to me about the politically correct thing -- you can make your point without looking down your nose at people.

I think of that contrast often now as I engage with progressives on listservs and Facebook. I think about it when I watch focus groups of people outside the Beltway talking politics, or when I go home to the Midwest and hang out in gossipy small-town diners. I believe progressives should be sensitive to everyone, treat everyone as they want to be treated, call everyone what they want to be called, and try very hard not to hurt people with the language we use. But I also believe that we need to build positive connections to people who hold many of the same values that we do, but who are not immersed in a day-to-day dialogue about the nuances – important as they are – of how we talk to one another.

A couple of examples. I know that many folks in the progressive space get upset when someone says "illegal immigrant" rather than "undocumented immigrant" -- and they should. There is no such thing as an illegal person, and progressives should push back against that kind of language. But many folks outside the Beltway don't know that it's problematic language, or they don't get the importance of the distinction when it is not considered problematic to say that a person "immigrated illegally." We need to be gentle with folks who think of it as a grammatical issue or a distinction without a difference.

Here's another. As a straight guy, I have worked hard to learn the nuances on how to talk about sexual orientation from my friends and movement colleagues who are not straight folks. I want to respect and fight for the rights of everyone, but the trend of adding all those new letters to LGBT has confused me. I was talking with Lauren Windsor, who is bisexual, about all this, and here was her take:

> Let's look at the ever-expanding acronym for the queer community: LGBT. Lesbian, gay, bisexual, and transgender. Then came Q for queer or questioning, I for intersex, and A for asexual or ally. LGBTQIA. In researching this part of the book, I found that Amherst College gave representation to all those groups with an LGBTQQIAA center, in a New York Times article from 2013. Sometime in the interim, Amherst dropped the double letters and added a P, for pansexual. Luckily, the name of the center is the Queer Resource Center, or they would have to be perennially changing all their stationary.

> The most current configuration seems to be LGBTQQIP2SAA: lesbian, gay, bisexual, transgender, questioning, queer, intersex, pansexual, two-spirit (2S), androgynous, and asexual. Now, I'm supportive of whatever gender identity and sexuality anyone has or wants to explore (so long as the sex is between consenting adults), but being from the South, I don't think it's realistic to expect that most folks there know the latest appropriate acronym. Or the meaning of 'cisgender.' (If you don't know, cisgender refers to anyone whose gender identity matches their sex at birth.) Or that they understand why you would include your preferred pronouns in your e-mail signature. This quest for inclusivity can, perversely, be alienating, even to the most enlightened liberals. Count me as one of them, and to underscore, I'm bisexual.

Language is deeply powerful, and deeply personal, and we need to keep moving toward less biased, less hateful and more inclusive ways of expressing ourselves. But we also need to look beneath the surface, find the things that tie us together, and save some of our judgment for a time when we have built the relationships needed to communicate directly and effectively about how things need to change. The feeling that progressives don't relate culturally to outside the Beltway folks hurts our cause more than any other thing going on right now.

The Challenge at the Heart of Everything: Racism

There is no more foundational dynamic in American culture and politics than racism. From our earliest days as a nation to the candidacy of Donald Trump, racists have been all too successful in American politics. For all the progress we have made since establishing the Voting and Civil Rights Acts, for all the pride liberals felt in electing a black son of an immigrant, Barack Obama, for all the racial diversity we have added in the last half-century, the centrality of racism is as true today as it was in the 1600s.

Democrats cannot survive without building a vibrant, cohesive, and enduring multi-racial coalition. The numbers just don't add up any other way. And that means three things:

- First, people of color aren't going to put up with excuses or settle for weak responses on issues concerning their communities anymore;

- Second, the corollary to the first point is that white Democrats need to get over the idea that we can still win strong support from people of color while softening our approach on key issues (cough, cough immigration);

- Third, notwithstanding the two points above, there needs to be genuine, ongoing dialogue between whites and people of color to come up with a common language, narrative, and strategy on approaching issues. We need to build a culture of mutual respect and genuine understanding, and this is why long-term organizing and relationship-building are so central to being able to win.

A lot of white Democrats these days are solemnly warning that we need to avoid this awful thing called "identity politics." They say we need to focus instead on more universal issues like economics. I never know how to respond to this kind of conversation. In fact, I have no frickin' clue what they are talking about. I say, yes, absolutely, let's focus on economic issues! That is most of what this book is about, and by the way, people of color care just as much about those universal economic issues as white folks do. But if "we shouldn't focus on identity politics" translates into not talking about issues like criminal justice reform or immigration that are central to the lives of people of color, I call bullshit. Because we have to. A fundamental charge of the Democratic Party is to care about fairness. It's part of our core identity, and our base will never, and should never, let us walk away from those important issues.

Bringing a substantial group of working-class white people into a long-term coalition with people of color will never be easy. But history shows this can be done. In the reconstruction era in the South, in the New Deal coalition and the 1960s coalition, in the 1990s and Obama's two presidential campaign victories, we saw glimpses of an enduring coalition that could work. And with the sectors of the electorate that are more likely to be progressive – especially people of color, young voters, and unmarried women – growing steadily, the potential is clearly there.

On a grassroots level, community and labor organizers have been successfully building durable, powerful multiracial coalitions for years. A great current example comes from my home state, Nebraska. Remember my friend Jane Kleeb? In addition to being the Chair of the Nebraska Democratic Party, she's one of the best organizers in the nation, having built what she sometimes refers to as the 'Cowboy & Indian Alliance.' Jane lives in Hastings, deep in the heart of cattle country, and her work bringing together ranchers and tribal leaders to fight pipeline construction on their lands in Nebraska and the Dakotas created a powerful center of gravity on the issue.

Younger generations are more diverse than ever before. Because the kids are more accustomed to having friends across racial lines, youth organizing groups have developed some great multiracial organizing models. This kind of coalition-building across racial lines will become easier as the years go by, and will make political messaging easier as well.

In the meantime, how should Democrats be talking to white working-class voters and people of color in a way that both groups will find compelling?

First, Democrats need to have both a universal track on economic issues and a specialized track when talking to different groups of voters. What I mean by this is that there is an economic message and agenda that will appeal strongly to the broad majority of working- and middle-class voters regardless of race or geography. That message, which I will talk about at more length later in the book, takes on trickledown economics that benefits the top 1%, Wall Street, and wealthy special interests, and rebuilds the American Dream in a fair way for working families. A solid plan for good jobs with good wages and benefits. This kind of message appeals to and motivates both Democratic base and swing voters across racial and geographic lines.

However, different groups of voters also need to hear messages addressing their own specific issues and needs. African-American and Latino voters need to hear tangible ideas to reform the criminal justice system. Young people need to hear about ideas to reduce the burden of student loan debt. Women need to hear ideas for protecting their reproductive health options and strengthening families. Rural voters need to hear Democrats addressing rural health care, schools, and infrastructure.

There is nothing surprising here. Voters always want politicians to tell them about their stands on issues specific to their communities, and most politicians are actually pretty good at being sensitive to those specific concerns. But most voters also want to hear about universal economic issues, and Democrats have too often in recent years forgotten to center those issues in their pitch.

I am firmly convinced that there are a great many working-class white folks who have no problem with Democrats talking about immigration and criminal justice issues -- many of whom in fact agree with us on those issues -- so long as we put economic issues at the heart of our message. On the other hand, if they don't know where we stand on economics, if we don't talk about economic issues enough or do it in a cautious, muddled way, too many white voters, manipulated by the racist appeals of right-wing

Republicans, will come to perceive that the only people we care about are immigrants and people of color.

The other key thing we need to remember as we build a multiracial strategy is that issues like criminal justice reform and immigration are fundamentally economic issues. Check out the for-profit prison industry and the economic exploitation of undocumented workers if you have any doubts on that score. There's a powerful idea that has been developed in academia called "intersectionality." It is the idea that racism, sexism, and classism are interconnected and that they create overlapping structures of discrimination. While I wouldn't advocate using the word intersectionality on the campaign trail, Democrats need to build a narrative around the concept. We need to weave economics together with these other issues in a way that's relatable for both people of color and whites.

It will never be easy for any political party that wants to build a robust multiracial coalition to navigate racism in America. But I am convinced that if we center our appeal to voters on universal ideas about a fairer economy, while weaving together other issues that matter the most to specific constituencies, we will be able to appeal to working-class folks across the board.

Bringing It All Together

This chapter has covered a lot of ground, examining strategic arguments and assumptions from a variety of Democrats. After reading a great deal of data and many well-written strategy papers, I am convinced that if we are going to succeed at creating a desperately needed, sustainable governing majority, we must make an all-out push in terms of communicating with, motivating, organizing, and turning out the vote of base Democratic groups, while at the same time winning considerably more working-class voters, especially in rural areas and small towns. In order to do both, we need to make a populist economic argument the center of our political message; to create a thoughtful and aggressive organizing and communications strategy to battle straightforwardly with racism and the central issues that matter to people of color; and to let go of the political correctness that creates a cultural division between progressives and working-class folks.

I will be the first to admit that this is a tall order. If it were easy, Republicans wouldn't have won so many elections over the last decade. Democrats have to move past their old strategic assumptions about who the most important swing voters are, and we have to stop creating a false choice between swing voters and our base. I know we can do this. To quote one famous Democratic unifier, "Yes we can."

CHAPTER FOUR: SMALL TOWN VALUES

I argued in the last chapter that a central part of winning a sustainable governing majority is appealing to working-class voters of all backgrounds and regions. Small-town and rural America are the parts of the country Democrats have the most trouble reaching; there just isn't that much party or progressive infrastructure there. In this chapter, I want to describe a messaging and organizing strategy that I believe can win back the small-town and rural voters we need.

I start with the understanding that Democrats are unlikely to ever win, at least in my lifetime and probably well after that, the majority of voters in rural America. We don't need to, of course. Assuming the exit polls were accurate, and based on vote totals coming back from more rural counties they probably were, Bill Clinton in 1996 and Barack Obama in 2008 both got as high as 45% in those areas while winning overall going away. We probably won't get much higher than that number any time soon. Given that the country's population is growing more urban and more diversified every year, we will always be in great shape if we only lose the countryside 55-45 in presidential elections.

But there is a big difference between losing in rural America 55-45 and only getting a third of the vote, as Hillary Clinton apparently did. Part of the reason for Clinton's low numbers was depressed Democratic turnout, but part of it was energized Republican turnout in opposition to her candidacy. You're in trouble if the folks who live in small towns dislike you so much that they turn out to vote for anyone but you, even if your opponent is a malignant narcissist. Obviously, Hillary Clinton came to the race with a lot of baggage particular to her, based on 30-plus years of Republican attacks. But the Democratic Party would be wise not to write her loss off as idiosyncratic, while continuing to replicate her campaign's mistakes.

Beyond the presidential race, we need to find candidates who can compete well enough in the countryside to win Senate and House seats in places like Montana and Kansas. Our ability as a party to do that has gotten more and more shaky in recent years, but it wasn't that long ago when we were doing quite a bit better in those environs. Not too long ago in the Senate, Montana was represented by Max Baucus and Jon Tester; North Dakota by Byron Dorgan and Kent Conrad; South Dakota by Tom Daschle and Tim Johnson; West Virginia by Jay Rockefeller and Robert Byrd; Nebraska by Ben Nelson; Arkansas by Blanche Lincoln and Mark Pryor; and Alaska by Mark Begich. Those are 12 Democratic Senators from seven small, rural states that are dark red in presidential elections. Today, only three of those seats are still represented by Democrats. All three of them are up this year and all are top targets for the GOP. We must be able to get some of these kinds of seats back.

I also want to make one point very strongly to all my progressive friends: if you don't care about the fates of the people who live in small towns and the countryside, I don't see how you can call yourself a progressive.

You care about poor people? A higher percentage of people in "the sticks" live in poverty than do in urban areas. You care about giving everyone quality education? Small-town schools are among the most dilapidated in the nation, many without computers or updated textbooks. You care about equal opportunity? Tens of millions of Americans in the countryside have no access to high-speed internet services or decent legal help if they get accused of a crime. You care about everyone having access to health care? Rural health care is the worst in the country by many measures. You care about mental health issues? Nowhere has been harder hit by the opioid epidemic than small towns. You care about creating jobs and raising wages? Rural America has terrible rates of job creation compared to metro areas, and the lowest wages in the country.

There's a reason people out there are pissed. We progressives need to reach out to them and get them on our side.

Myths About Rural America

1. **Everyone out there is white.** While the countryside is whiter than urban America, there are plenty of people of color there, millions of them. In fact, 20.4% of rural/small-town Americans are people of color. Given that rural people of color tend to be quite poor; are rarely targeted in the urban-oriented GOTV operations of the Democratic Party; and are usually not much connected to the white majority's civic society, their voter turnout rates tend to be abysmally low.

In the 2016 election, in the closing weeks of the campaign, I got a call from my friend Lazar Palnick in Pittsburgh, and he told me that there were no plans by the state party or the Clinton campaign to do GOTV in the African-American neighborhoods in the small towns of Pennsylvania, or even big city suburbs -- all of the Democratic GOTV operations related to African-Americans were concentrated in inner city Philly and Pittsburgh. He, I, and a couple of other folks tried to scrape together the money to make that happen. We got partway there but couldn't fully fund the project. If we had found the money, we might well have swung Pennsylvania for Clinton and the Democratic Senate candidate Katie McGinty. That kind of story is replicated in state after state, election after election.

Another example is the situation in Nebraska, where the Latino population has skyrocketed from 1% when I was growing up to around 12% today (the 2010 census had the number as 10.3%, but the explosive growth in this population has continued throughout the decade). A lot of the rural Nebraska counties are 25% or more Latino. Hall County, where Grand Island is, now has a Latino population of over 40%; Scottsbluff, way out west, over 25%; the small town of Lexington, in the middle of the state, over 50%. But these big numbers are not backed up by a GOTV operation, since the Democratic county parties tend to be led by older white people who have never connected with the mostly unregistered Latino population.

American Indian reservations are another place where registration and turnout numbers are very low. Voter registration drives and GOTV drives on reservations in western states can make a huge difference in close elections -- several of those western state senators I mentioned a minute ago would never have won their elections without a big GOTV operation in Indian country. But in most elections, there is very little done to turn out the Indian vote.

Think about how much easier it would be to improve Democrats' percentage in rural America if we just paid attention to the people of color who lived there.

2. **There are no lefties in rural America.** This is a favorite argument of conservative-leaning Democrats who claim that we can't afford to go too far left because we will not do well enough in rural America. But this stereotype is as wrong as "the countryside is all white" myth.

Look at the heavily rural states that Bernie Sanders won in the 2016 primaries: Alaska, Idaho, Kansas, Maine, Montana, Nebraska, North Dakota, Oklahoma, Utah, West Virginia. And most of the other states he won were Midwestern -- Indiana, Michigan, Minnesota, and Wisconsin -- with some big cities, but lots of rural turf, where Sanders did well.

People from MoveOn, Daily Kos, DFA, Indivisible, and other progressive online groups all tell me they have very active engagement and membership in many small counties and states across the country.

Take it from me, as a Nebraskan who grew up in a small, very Republican state: when you become a Democrat in that kind of state, you have some passion and gumption in your soul -- you have to, in order to survive. We can do a better job as a party and progressive movement in targeting rural areas, and these kinds of progressives are exactly the kind of people we need to be recruiting.

Another reason that Hillary did so poorly in rural America was that 25% of Bernie primary voters didn't vote for her. If you lived in the sticks and you were a Bernie person, you had two reasons to feel ignored and alienated.

3. **Social issues like guns, abortion, and LGBT rights drive the politics of rural America.** Polling is conclusive on this issue: rural folks vote primarily on economic issues, not on the stereotypical hot button social issues. Given the levels of poverty, lower wages, and problems with rural health care and education, this is not a big surprise.

Attitudes on social issues do tend to be somewhat more conservative than in urban areas, but not radically so. For example, a lot more people in rural areas than in urban areas own guns (mainly hunting rifles), but they don't generally own assault weapons and are fine with background checks to make sure criminals and dangerous, mentally ill people don't get guns. Only the most hard-core NRA people vote exclusively on the gun issue.

Don't forget my earlier points about Bill Clinton and Barack Obama: despite their liberal stands on social issues, despite the attacks from the NRA and Christian Coalition-style groups, they were able to do relatively well in small towns and rural areas in at least one election. Bill Clinton won West Virginia, Tennessee, Kentucky, Missouri, and Arkansas, after signing two gun-control bills. He prevailed because we kept talking to the folks in the countryside. Four years later, Al Gore was scared to talk about guns in rural America. He left the field to the NRA, and subsequently lost all those states. If we take progressive stands on issues like guns, we have to go explain to rural folks why we did. If we engage in that way, plenty of those voters will agree with us. There is no reason to think that being a progressive on these issues dooms us.

Just to underscore, if Democrats leave the field and don't engage with people in rural America on why we believe what we believe, groups like the NRA and the Christian conservative groups will be the only ones talking with voters about the issues.

4. **You have to turn mushy on issues like immigration and criminal justice reform to do well in rural America.** Again, how exactly does a black man, the son of an African immigrant with an African-Muslim name, do as well as any Democrat in modern times in rural America in 2008 if progressive attitudes about race make it impossible to do well in the countryside?

It is true that there is some deep-seated racism in the small towns of this country (just like there are in suburbs and big cities), and that we will lose some votes in rural America if we take strong stands on issues that particularly affect people of color. But mostly, those are not votes we were going to win anyway. For those genuinely swing-y white voters in rural America we would lose by taking strong stands on those issues, there are plenty of other votes we could go and get. Not only could we more than make up for those losses with increased people-of-color enthusiasm in urban areas, but we might even make up the numbers in rural counties by turning out more of the people of color who live there and are usually ignored. I also think that if we offer the full package of good political outreach to rural America with an overall agenda that voters like, we will still get more of their support even if they don't agree with us on everything.

Winning Hearts and Minds in the Countryside

A part of improving our percentage in rural America is increasing the voter turnout of the people of color who live there. Part of it is energizing the Bernie-oriented progressive populists who won so many rural states and counties for him in the 2016 primaries, but didn't turn out in big numbers in the general election. Part of it, frankly, is just showing up. If we ignore rural voters, they are much more likely to reject us, especially since they already assume Democrats don't care much about them.

But there's another part to the strategy as well: talking about the values and issues that have substantive and cultural resonance with people who live in rural areas and small towns.

Every place to live has its pros and cons. Small towns are no exception. But the good thing about them is the sense of community. Everyone knows each other, and people really care about the local institutions and how their neighbors are doing. When people get sick, folks all over town pitch in money to help pay medical bills. When older people start to have more trouble taking care of themselves, people drop by with groceries or just to check in. When there is a wedding or new baby, everyone shares in the joy. When there is tragedy, everyone comes to the funeral and brings food for the family.

I don't want to claim that life in rural areas and small towns is idyllic. I have seen plenty of prejudice, small-mindedness, and petty gossip there, too. If I never have to listen to another conversation in a small-town café about who did and didn't get to church on Sunday, I will die a happy man. But the sense of community is a blessing and something Democrats and progressives want to foster in society as a whole. We want to live in a country where people are good neighbors, where people pitch in and help lift each other up. And in our political language, this is what we want to be talking about to small-town folks.

A second key small-town value is self-reliance. Folks know that sometimes people need help -- everybody has rough patches for whatever reason -- but they value being able to take care of themselves and their families. Democrats need to emphasize that we want to build a society where we empower people to be more independent. A good education, decent health care, good jobs and living wages, markets not dominated by a few big businesses that allow for small businesses to compete. This is all about giving working people a chance to have a better life, a life where they can support their families and rely less on the government safety net.

A third thing that tends to matter more to small-town voters is tradition. Conservatives preach a lot about traditional American values, but there is nothing traditional about Donald Trump or the radical agenda he and other Republicans are pursuing. They want to tear down the society we built in the 20th century, and turn America into a place where the cronies of the government can do anything they want, regardless of decency or even the rule of law.

Democrats stand in opposition to the values driving Trump and his cronies, and we need to talk more about the traditional American values we believe in. The freedom to build a good life for yourself and your family. Making sure that our kids have the tools to grow up strong and safe, so they can find their way as adults. Ensuring that senior citizens have enough support to live with dignity. Protecting workers and consumers from being cheated by the rich and powerful, so that our society remains fair and decent to all its citizens. Strengthening our communities and helping each other when the hard times come. Those are the kinds of values and traditions people in rural America, as well as urban America, believe in and support.

Finally, people in rural America value freedom above all. I will write at length later about this word, and the competing definitions for it between progressives and conservatives. For now, I want to note how much people in small towns and rural America value the freedom to make their own decisions and raise their families in their own way. Most Americans long ago migrated to urban areas, where there were more jobs and better pay, better schools, better health care. You've got to be a bit stubborn to stay in rural America, kind of against the grain, and it gives you a certain attitude. Part of why rural folks value freedom so much, and part of why they are skeptical of government, is that they just don't want to be told what to do or how to do it. What Democrats need to make clear is that the government we advocate for will make it possible for people to have more, not less, freedom to live the way they want.

An Economic Agenda for Small-Town America

My friends at the Center for Community Change (CCC), one of the biggest organizations in the country working on issues impacting low-income people, have long argued that a progressive economic agenda should explicitly include a focus on creating jobs and raising incomes among those who are poorest. That seems like common sense, but remarkably has not always been spelled out by Democrats when they talk about their economic policies.

We need this kind of targeted economic investment in rural America, as well as urban America. Here are some things

Democrats can do as part of an economic program for small towns
and rural areas:

1. **Address transportation and energy infrastructure needs**.
   Having spent an enormous amount of time on the
   backcountry roads of this great nation, I can tell you I've
   traveled on a lot of scary bridges and beat up roads. When
   Obama's stimulus plan went into place, and a lot of those
   roads and bridges were improved, it made a big difference in
   people's daily lives. When you invest in better roads, you
   make it easier for small businesses in small towns to get their
   goods to market.

   And it's really absurd that we have not invested substantially
   in high-speed electric rail. It may not be economically feasible
   to build everywhere in America yet (certainly not on the scale
   of Asia with its high population density), but that has been an
   issue for many major infrastructure and economic
   development projects. Yes, improving our train systems will
   benefit big cities, but it will also benefit the rural areas and
   small towns in between, not to mention our environment.

   Speaking of which, transitioning our power plants to
   renewable energy should be a top priority. We can reduce our
   dependence on fossil fuels, their emissions, and the cost of
   energy, plus provide job retraining for unemployed coal
   miners and manufacturing workers. Government subsidy is
   critical for launching the next wave of innovation, whether
   that's the internet, medical research and development, high
   speed trains, or renewable energy.

2. **Upgrade internet access.** Nothing will do more to spur
   economic development in rural America than universal
   broadband. If people in small towns and on farms have access
   to the same high speed technology as their urban
   counterparts, entrepreneurialism will be sparked. One early
   adopter of this technology at a municipal level was
   Chattanooga, TN, which created a taxpayer-owned gigabit
   fiber-optic network that is credited with transforming the city
   into a vibrant tech hub.

3. **Repair and build new schools.** Repairing and rebuilding the rundown schools in much of rural America would not only improve education for small town kids, it would create hundreds of thousands of jobs.

4. **Improve health care.** One of the clearest differences between Democrats and Republicans in terms of improving the lives of people in rural America is the Affordable Care Act's investment in rural health care. The states that have chosen Medicaid expansion have found that those policies also dramatically help rural hospitals. Given the importance of health care to the economy and the state of health care resources in rural America, making these kinds of investments in rural health care is essential. Especially in the Rust Belt and Coal Country, where many states have been devastated by job loss and the opioid crisis.

In 2017, Pennsylvania Governor Tom Wolf warned that more than 670,000 people would lose coverage in his state if the Trump administration succeeded in repealing Medicaid expansion under the ACA. It's a damn shame that Democrats did not full-throatedly defend and promote Obamacare in 2014 and 2016. Many folks just didn't realize how much they had gained under the law, until it was nearly snatched away from them under a GOP Congress. Had Democrats not been so cowardly, perhaps we'd have seen different electoral outcomes in states like Pennsylvania.

5. **Invest in solving the opioid crisis.** This is an economic issue as well as a heartbreaking social issue. A major investment by drug companies and the federal government to solve this problem would make many lives and communities whole again. It would lead to new productivity and new entrepreneurship. And the jobs created by making this kind of investment would matter a lot to small communities.

6. **Support small business development.** Targeted programs to help spur small business development would be an enormous boon to local economies. Tens of thousands of

local retail shops in small towns have been shuttered over the last few decades because of the monopoly power of Wal-Mart and Amazon. Big businesses have made local entrepreneurialism harder and harder. Creating more small business-spurring centers in small towns across the country, preferably based in community colleges, has the potential to create a large number of new jobs.

7. **Sustain family farms**. Most family farms have disappeared in the last several decades, as they have been either bought out or crushed by Big Ag conglomerates. Farmers are now less than 1% of the population, and many that remain are big factory farms. But smaller family farms still exist, and government should be on their side against the monopolistic Big Ag factory farms that drive their crop and animal prices down. Additionally, the growing demand for organic food opens up new market opportunities for these farmers, which should be supported by government policy.

8. **Invest in bio-based manufacturing.** Tom Vilsack has been a leading advocate for policies to support bio-based manufacturing his entire career, and his argument is one that should resonate with progressives. Tom says we need to move away from the extractive industries that have dominated the rural economy historically. Instead, we should move toward building a sustainable economy turning plants, crops, and animal wastes into a wide variety of manufacturing materials: chemicals, fabrics, fibers, fuels, and energy.

9. **Develop local and regional food systems.** This is another idea that Vilsack has been promoting aggressively. According to Tom, "Today, more than 160,000 family farmers have decided to stop playing the commodity game and have begun to develop their own local and regional markets. The benefit of this is that in a local and regional market, the farmer dictates the price." It also happens to be more efficient and better for the environment.

Showing Up

Much of politics is just showing up, and Democrats haven't done much of that in rural America in recent years. We haven't been campaigning very much in small towns, and we don't talk much about rural and small-town America when we do campaign. Our language and culture feels very foreign to the people who live there. As Van Jones has eloquently spoken to in his books, speeches, and TV commentary, some urban progressives are downright disdainful of those folks who live in "the sticks."

It is going to take a serious investment of time and effort to show rural folks that we care about them. Democrats need to start showing up again. We need to campaign in small towns and meet with farmers; to have an agenda that includes and embraces the countryside; to talk about the kind of small-town community values we want to guide our country.

Democrats should do this because it is the right thing to do. No part of this country should be ignored, and the problems of rural Americans are as bad as those of any other demographic group in the country. But we should also do it for purely pragmatic reasons. If we start getting 45% of the rural vote again, instead of the third of the vote we now get in a lot of elections, we will gain majorities in Congress, and win Senate and House races in many small, red states that currently aren't electing Democrats.

CHAPTER FIVE: PRO-BUSINESS DEMOCRATS

As the party promoting justice, equal rights, labor, progressive taxation, environmentalism, and an appropriate role for government, Democrats -- especially progressive Democrats -- have always had a bit of a tortured relationship with the world of business. Because we want to prevent unfettered corporate hegemony, our relationship with business was always bound to be a little edgy. But contrary to the rants of conservative pundits, Democrats have never been "anti-business."

You can be a Democrat and be pro-business. In fact, progressive Democratic policies are far better for the vast majority of businesses – especially small business and entrepreneurs – than those with either a Republican or a more big business-inclined Democratic orientation. And to my progressive brothers and sisters, I want to emphasize how politically important it is that we remind voters of how good our policy ideas are for small businesses and other good business actors.

Let me start this chapter by taking a step back and talking about the political and policy decisions made in the Bill Clinton presidency.

Being Pro-Business in the Bill Clinton Years

When Bill Clinton ran for and won the presidency, he was determined to be seen as a "New Democrat." Part of the newness in his mind was having a pro-business outlook. He strongly believed that old-school Democrats had been too pro-government, and that the voters had soured on the public sector. While Clinton supported some old-school Democratic ideas like universal health care, a cleaner environment, more spending on education, affirmative action, and a higher minimum wage, he also believed that you could do all of that and still make government more in tune with markets and business.

Originally that translated into a heavier emphasis on small business. A sign of how important small business was to Clinton was that his first two Small Business Administration directors, Erskine Bowles and Phil Lader, were very close friends who also served at different points as chief of staff and deputy chief of staff. Another sign was that when we were working on health care reform, we put a huge amount of emphasis on structuring the bill to maximize the benefits and minimize the costs to small business.

Progressives like me who served in the Clinton administration, while not comfortable with some of the "pro-business" stuff Clinton was doing, were mostly okay with the tradeoff because we had no problem with helping small business, and it seemed like we were getting quite a bit of what we wanted, too. For example, in the budget fight in 1993, we got a budget that included higher taxes on the wealthy, lower taxes on the poor, and lots of investment in programs that we supported. In the big budget fights with a Republican Congress later in the 1990s, Clinton went to the mat for Medicare, Medicaid, education, and the environment, and we even out-maneuvered (in partnership with Teddy Kennedy) the Republican leadership to get the Children's Health Insurance Program and a higher minimum wage passed.

As the years went on, though, with the Republican-controlled Congress and Clinton's love of making deals, the pro-Big Business part of the policy program became a much more significant problem for progressive-minded folks. Trade deals like NAFTA and allowing China into the WTO never benefitted working people much despite promises that they would. The Telecom Act of 1996 allowed the merger of Big Media companies into monster-sized media conglomerates. The 1999 financial deregulation bill repealed Glass-Steagall, taking down the wall between commercial and investment banking, and allowed the creation of a small number of enormous banks that became known as "Too-Big-to-Fail" during the financial collapse of 2008. And the DOJ's Anti-Trust division never returned to the pre-Reagan level of assertiveness in terms of keeping corporations from growing so big that they squashed their smaller competitors.

The Obama Administration's Continuation of Clinton's Economic Policies

Bill Clinton's policies regarding business mostly carried over into the Obama years, which later caused many progressive Democrats to view Hillary's 2016 positions on Wall Street and trade as suspect. Under Obama, the Too-Big-to-Fail banks got bailed out and then got even bigger, and their executives got to keep their bonuses instead of going to jail for the crimes that caused the sub-prime mortgage meltdown. Obama had talked tough on banks, but his Department of Justice (DOJ) had no bite – top officials like Attorney General Eric Holder publicly admitted to considering the impact of prosecuting bankers of big firms on the financial markets, essentially arguing that they were Too-Big-to-Jail. Hillary infamously gave $400k speeches to Goldman Sachs, which hurt her badly with both progressives and with working-class swing voters.

Obama's trade deals, like the now-dead Trans-Pacific Partnership (TPP), were still more focused on giving big corporations what they wanted, rather than helping workers and consumers. Despite the TPP's unpopularity, Obama continued promoting it throughout the 2016 cycle, causing Hillary considerable heartburn. She opposed it during her campaign, but Obama undercut her credibility on the issue by continuing to campaign for it.

Donald Trump ran to the left of Clinton on both Wall Street and trade, and he won, in part, on this progressive populist message. Elizabeth Warren was saying that "the system is rigged" back in 2009, and Bernie Sanders made that the mantra of his campaign. But it was Trump that won with it because the Hillary campaign did not want to take up the mantle of populism. Even her mild admonitions of Wall Street were not believable to voters, who saw her as the embodiment of the establishment.

Additionally under Obama, the DOJ's Anti-Trust division remained quiet while one company after another grew to market-distorting size and crushed or bought out their competitors. Corporations with the size and power of Facebook, Amazon, and Wal-Mart developed concentrated power in one economic sector after the next, distorting markets and crushing competitors, workers, and consumers alike.

Being pro-business for Democrats had morphed into being pro-Big Business. This was not only bad policy, but it wreaked electoral havoc on our party. Those who didn't raise more hell about this in the 1990s, myself included, were wrong. It is deeply ironic to me that I spent most of my energy in 1998 and early '99 helping to lead the fight against Clinton's impeachment, while doing little to stop the repeal of Glass-Steagall, which was going on at the same time. (Now I spend much of my time fighting for Wall Street reform with the likes of Elizabeth Warren, Sherrod Brown, and Jeff Merkley.) While I still think opposing impeachment was the right thing to do, I would not make the same choices again.

As we see the backlash toward the Democratic Party that these pro-Big Business policies of the last 25 years have helped spawn, Democrats need to rethink the way they approach business. My central argument here is this: Democrats and progressives should reject the strategy of being close to Big Business and replace it with policies and messaging that are pro-small business, pro-responsible business, pro-entrepreneurialism, and pro-open, competitive markets. This stance is far better from a policy point of view and at the same time far better politically.

Why Progressive Democrats Tend to Be Better for Business

The more bottom-up (or middle-out, as progressive business leader Nick Hanauer likes to call it) approach Democrats tend to favor has always done far better for the economy than the Republican alternative. Dating back to Herbert Hoover, every single Republican president's policies have led us into serious recessions by the end of their time in office. Their tenures have consistently seen worse job growth, higher deficits, and worse stock market results than those of Democratic presidents.

The reason that Democratic policies historically have done better is that trickle-down economics -- giving more money to rich people in tax cuts in hopes they will invest it and create jobs -- isn't effective, while progressive policies make the overall economy run better and help most businesses make more money. There is literally no evidence in American history that trickle-down economics works very well.

The conventional wisdom is that conservative Republican policies are pro-business: low taxes, regulation, and wages, and fewer empowered workers. These things sound good in the short term, and for some kinds of businesses, they are very lucrative.

On balance, though, progressive Democratic policies are better for most businesses, especially those that are honest and ethical. Workers with higher wages and retirees with good retirement benefits have the money in their pocketbook to buy more products. Think Henry Ford paying his workers enough money, so that they could afford to buy his cars.

A better health care system that covers everyone, lowers costs, and invests in preventive care is cheaper for employers and reduces sick days and turnover. Think about how big an administrative and financial burden health care is on employers, especially small businesses. Why should businesses have to shoulder it? If we had a system where workers were covered by Medicare, businesses would be freed to focus on their core activities: selling their goods and services.

A stronger and better-funded public education system leads to a more productive and innovative workforce. More investments in infrastructure reduce the cost of bringing goods to market. Universal broadband gives workers more tools and makes the whole economy more entrepreneurial. Expanded investment in research and development advances technology and promotes innovation throughout the economy.

Perhaps most importantly of all, progressives believe in a level playing field and a cop on the beat (to borrow a phrase from Elizabeth Warren) who will keep the biggest, wealthiest, greediest, and most powerful businesses from cheating their competitors and dominating marketplaces. Vigorous antitrust enforcement and a general government bias toward small business and start-ups, instead of the insider cronies who look for sweetheart deals from government, help the vast majority of businesses.

Monopoly Power

I wrote this in 2014, but it's even truer today:

Here are two headlines from the Washington Post business pages the other day, lined up side by side on the page:

"Strong Earnings Send Stocks To New High"

and

"US Middle Class Still Suffering Amid Economic Recovery"

...the two headlines above tell the story of an economy — and a society — where the priorities are completely screwed up. This is not how you build a healthy sustainable economy. And remember, this is an economy that is officially four years into recovery, with a Democratic president who ran on a platform of fighting for the middle class. The fact that this economy is so lopsidedly in favor of the top 1 percent is not the result of a short-term glitch in the economy; it is not something we will grow our way out of. Tinkering will not make the changes we need... We are going to have to recognize the big things going on in the economy that must be addressed, the things that are foundational to the economic situation we find ourselves in.

We have to understand that we are living in an era where not only is wealth concentrated, but entire sectors of industry are becoming so concentrated as to be near-monopolies. The pioneering work of Barry Lynn in his book Cornered: The New Monopoly Capitalism and the Economics of Destruction, and in numerous other articles he and his colleagues at Open Markets Institute have written, documents this trend — and its terrible impact on our entire economy and society — in industry after industry. Everyone knows that Wal-Mart has become the dominant retailer in the country, that Amazon dominates the book industry and other forms of online commerce, that a few banks have become Too-Big-to-Fail, that there are fewer and fewer airlines. But what Lynn's work has documented is how this trend toward consolidation, concentration, and near-monopoly power has taken over industry after industry, and how this fact has been crushing entrepreneurialism and has warped our economy in a hundred different ways. The DOJ stopped enforcing most of the antitrust laws during the Reagan administration, and no administration since, Republican or Democrat, has picked up the task to any significant degree. We are all paying the price, and it is an incredibly steep one.

Lynn and his colleagues are required reading for anyone who wants to understand how monopolies and oligopolies are crushing competition and much of business in America. New business start-ups have been lagging behind for a couple of decades now, and modern-day monopolists are putting the old robber barons to shame.

More and more folks are starting to realize the enormity of the problem. Elizabeth Warren has been taking the political lead on the monopoly issue. She gave a speech in 2017 to the Open Markets Institute, where she said this:

> To rebuild an economy that works for everyone, not just the big guys, it is critical to reduce concentrated power in our markets. The federal government has the tools to do it. Congress handed antitrust enforcers those tools over a century ago. But those tools have been sitting on the shelf for decades, gathering dust.

In addition to blocking mergers that would create companies so big that they distort markets, Warren advocated that every single agency of government be assigned the task of looking into what would stop monopolies and oligopolies from developing and hurting market competition. This idea borrows from the New Deal era, when a variety of government agencies vigorously helped smaller and newer businesses that were getting crushed by the big boys.

Taking on monopolies helps pretty much everyone except, obviously, the monopoly itself. When consumers have more choices, they are less likely to see prices go up and services get cut. When their companies aren't so dominant, workers have more bargaining power. When industry isn't so concentrated in a few places, more cities and states have businesses as pillars of their community. When giant companies have less political and market power, taxpayers are less likely to get ripped off. If industry concentration is dispersed, more businesses have the chance to compete and flourish.

What progressives need to understand is how important open markets and competition are to the flowering of progressive goals, especially stopping the biggest businesses from dominating both our economy and our democracy. We need smaller and newer companies to compete and take market share from the big dogs. Without that competition, those big dogs just keep getting bigger, and their bite gets more vicious than ever.

Break Up the Motherfucking Banks

Speaking of Elizabeth Warren, nothing would be more pro-business than lessening the power of Wall Street's grip on the American economy. Another thing I wrote back in 2014 is even truer today:

> The financialization of the economy is weakening the entire middle class. The Too-Big-to-Fail banks are 30 percent bigger than they were in 2008, and the industry increasingly takes a higher and higher share of both total corporate profits and the entire economy. Financial services as a share of the economy has tripled since 1950. Compensation in the financial industry used to be about the same as that of other industries, but since 1980, it has skyrocketed and is now 70 percent more on average. Financial services now make up more than 40 percent of all corporate profits in this country. What all this means is that a very small number of bankers are now hoarding more and more of the money circulating in the economy. And it's not like they are investing in mom-and-pop start-ups, either: more and more of the money is going into speculative trades and overseas investment, and less and less into entrepreneurs trying to start a new business.

For Senator Warren and other strong progressives like Sherrod Brown, who is the ranking Democrat on the Senate Banking Committee, taking on the power of Wall Street is at the heart of not only a progressive economic agenda, but a strong pro-small business and pro-open markets agenda. I know a lot of small business people, and have been one myself for close to two decades. I know no one who would prefer to do business with the big banks on Wall Street rather than local, community-based banks.

When Clinton made the big mistake of deregulating the financial services industry, especially with the repeal of Glass-Steagall, he consolidated an industry with a potential to create all kinds of problems. Unregulated financial speculation led directly to the housing bubble, which led directly to the worst financial panic and recession since The Great Depression, which was awful for everyone, and sure wasn't great for business. It led to millions of lost jobs, millions of foreclosed homes, and millions of small business failures.

If we break up the big banks; separate commercial banking from the riskier world of investment banking; and lessen the big banks' power over our economic and political system, our overall economy will be safer and more stable, and fewer consumers of all kinds, small businesses included, will get cheated. But arguably the biggest single beneficiary of all this will be the millions of businesses that don't have to kowtow to Wall Street to get loans or investment dollars.

A quick story: I believe that the central story of politics is who has power and who doesn't. The reason I have been (and people like Warren and Brown have been) so focused on Wall Street in recent years isn't because of the bloodlust for revenge, as my old boss Bill Clinton once described populists' animus toward the big banks. It is because of the immense power they wield over the very heart of our economy. When banks become so big and so dominant that their greed can bring down the whole economy, it is time to break them up.

Early in the financial crisis, I was at a strategy retreat for financial reform activists. We were in a circle where everyone had been assigned to tell what their top policy goal was in terms of financial reform. Most people were being pretty wonky with specific policy proposals -- a financial transaction tax, auditing the Federal Reserve or restructuring its discount window, abolishing carried interest, etc. When it came to be my turn, I just said, "break up the motherfucking banks," because I think the big banks' size and power is at the heart of all of our financial industry problems. One of the key organizers who was there was author and activist Zephyr Teachout, and she was so delighted with my answer that she sent me a "Break Up the Motherfucking Banks" t-shirt, which I still wear with pride.

Promoting the Best Businesses and Industries

Another aspect of thinking about Democrats and business is that we need to openly promote and help businesses and industries that we think are the best for the American public.

Republicans who worship the unfettered free market above all other things rail against "government picking winners and losers," but government always has and always will pick winners and losers. The free market is a fallacy because a truly free market requires anarchy: markets require rules. Every nation in the world makes economic rules that benefit favored businesses, and the history of our own country is full of such examples. As we speak, fossil fuel energy companies get huge tax breaks and other subsidies; defense contractors get bids based directly on relationships with generals and politicians; agribusiness companies get tens of billions of dollars in payouts from the Treasury every year; Wall Street gets tax subsidies and special favors galore; cronies of Trump get one government contract after another. And so on and so on...

What government should be doing is assuring that neither cronyism nor the so-called free market decide on their own. We should openly acknowledge that some businesses and industries are better for our citizenry and actively promote them.

The biggest example that comes to mind is fostering green energy companies over the fossil fuel industry. Solar and wind jobs have exceeded those in oil and coal for some time. According to a 2017 report from the Department of Energy, solar power generation accounted for more jobs than oil, coal, and gas combined. For the sake of reducing climate change and other pollutants bad for our health, and for the sake of creating millions of new jobs, we should be doing everything we can to speed this trend along. From a carbon tax on fossil fuel use, to big new tax subsidies for renewables, to mandates requiring the transition to renewables in the electric grid and the manufacture of electric vehicles, and everything in between, we should be doing all we can to help launch hundreds of thousands of new small businesses that will help us make the transition to a carbon-free future.

You want to know a few other kinds of businesses worthy of progressive and government support and promotion? More locally owned businesses owned by people of color serving communities of color. Modest-sized family farms. Mom-and-pop grocery stores and retailers. Small tech start-ups that might someday be able to compete with the tech giants. Banks and credit unions that are genuinely local and community-based instead of the $250 billion conglomerates that make this claim. Locally owned bookstores, newspapers, radio stations, coffee shops, and restaurants. Up-and-coming artists and art galleries. And thousands of other local and start-up businesses that can serve as engines of growth and pillars of their communities.

Plenty of more sizable businesses are good corporate citizens, and as Democrats, we should herald them as well. No matter their size, if businesses pay their workers a decent wage and provide good benefits; do their best to minimize their carbon footprint and other pollution; don't engage in union bashing; don't discriminate against certain classes of people or neighborhoods; and don't cheat on their taxes or cheat their competitors, they should be recognized and supported. I have many friends in business who run ethical, responsible companies and are very successful. Progressives should patronize these kinds of companies, and Democrats should hold them up as examples of the types of business we support. On the other hand - and most of my friends in business strongly agree with this notion - big businesses don't generally need extra subsidies or tax write-offs from government. (For example, there's a great organization made of businesspeople and other wealthy folks called Patriotic Millionaires that calls for higher taxes on the wealthy, increased wages, and other progressive economic policies.)

The Political Benefits of Being Aligned with Small Business

Democrats would do well to talk more about how our policy ideas are good for business, especially small business. If voters perceive that they must make a choice between healthy businesses and economic growth on the one hand, and fairness and economic equity on the other, while they like the latter, a lot of them will probably choose the former. But the fact is that this is another false choice. We need to talk about how Democratic and progressive policies can and do achieve both goals.

Something important to keep in mind is that there is no more revered institution in the minds of American voters than small business. This is why the Chamber of Commerce and the GOP always talk about the benefits to smaller companies when trying to sell voters on conservative economic policy. Democrats should spend a lot more time doing the same for progressive policy.

Additionally, Democrats and progressive leaders should spend far more time reaching out to and organizing small business leaders to be a part of their political coalition. My friends at MoveOn.org tell me that they have more than 30,000 active members who have indicated on surveys that they are small business people. We should be making more of an effort to build a large, engaged small business movement that will promote progressive economic policy.

Several good, progressive small business groups currently exist, including the American Sustainable Business Council, the Main Street Alliance, and the Small Business Majority. These organizations have provided an important counter narrative to the far right-wing voices of the Chamber of Commerce, the National Federation of Independent Businesses, and the National Restaurant Association. Democrats would be far better served to court and support these groups over Big Business lobbies.

Progressive Democrats who are fighting on a range of social and economic justice issues sometimes fall into the same thought pattern of right-wing politicians and media: that Republicans are the party of business and Democrats are the party of fairness. We need to reject that false choice: it is our progressive movement and Democratic Party whose policies are best for both business and fairness. The bottom line is that being progressive is good for business.

CHAPTER SIX: DRAINING THE SWAMP AND BUILDING A HOUSE

The progressive movement's resistance to the Donald Trump presidency has been awe-inspiring. This time will go down in the annals of American history as a critical moment when progressive leaders stood tall against a depraved demagogue and -- we all hope -- took him down. The grassroots-organized Women's March was, according to the Washington Post, likely the "largest single-day demonstration in recorded U.S. history" -- even more remarkable in its contrast to the paltry turnout for Trump's Inauguration just the day before. Thousands of people flooded to airports across the country to protest the Muslim ban. The yearlong, sustained fight to keep the Affordable Care Act alive kept Republicans from dismantling health care for millions of Americans.

The weekly demonstrations and lawsuits and petition drives made me proud. A lot of terrible things have happened and will happen in this country because Donald Trump is president, but all of this activism is reducing the damage and increasing political engagement among folks who would otherwise not be paying attention.

Our collective resistance has had a big effect, including on elections. Democratic turnout in the off-year elections of 2017 and the early elections of 2018 has consistently been higher than usual, and higher than Republican turnout in those races. Based on Democratic voter enthusiasm alone, 2018 could very well bring a big blue wave.

Grab 'Em by the Midterms

Unlike some Democrats, though, I don't believe that resistance to Trump is enough. There have been plenty of D.C. pundits who have said that we should just let Trump self-destruct, and not risk having a bold issue agenda that might upset anyone. But remember, this is the guy who said, "grab 'em by the pussy," and still won. Sidebar, when news of this broke, Lauren was apoplectic. She and her girlfriends made #NotMyPussy signs in protest at a local happy hour, for their personal Instagram feeds.

On the left, many progressive groups have made resisting Trump everything they talk about because that's what brings in online contributions and social media engagement. But I don't think we can just be anti-Trump and still win in the long term. Ronald Reagan and George W. Bush were terrible presidents and they both won re-election, Reagan in a landslide and Bush by a popular vote margin that shocked a lot of people. If all we are is anti-Trump, we can still have a solid year in 2018, but we won't be maximizing the wave for a potential tsunami. And if all we are is anti-Trump for four years, I don't believe we will win the presidency back.

One thing Democrats need to always remember: Trump's biggest single selling point is that he is shaking up the D.C. status quo. Many people are so desperate for change in our government that they are willing to burn this place down to achieve it. We underestimated that impulse to our own peril in 2016, by running too many safe, cautious candidates. We ought not replicate that mistake going forward. Many people think that Trump's ad hoc governance-by-tweet is authentic and a refreshing contrast to the canned, overly focus-grouped messaging of career politicos of either party.

Trump says what he thinks, regardless of whether it's true. His trademark "draining the swamp" rhetoric is the very embodiment of Orwellian doublespeak. Trump has hired more creepy swamp creatures than any president in history, and the stench of corruption is so thick you have to wade through it here in D.C.

Take for example, former South Carolina Congressman Mick Mulvaney, now Trump's budget director, who also runs the Consumer Financial Protection Bureau (CFPB), an agency he crusaded against as a legislator. Mulvaney recently told a conference of bankers that as a congressman it was his policy to only take meetings with lobbyists who donated to his campaign. He advised them to increase their donations to politicians in order to get them to destroy the CFPB. Just to underscore, Mulvaney explicitly advocated pay-to-play, so that bankers could crush an agency devoted to protecting consumers.

Then there's Scott Pruitt, Trump's Administrator for the Environmental Protection Agency (EPA) and a favorite of the oil billionaire Koch brothers. He's faced a barrage of ethics scandals from indulging in extensive, expensive first-class travel, to installing a $43k soundproof booth to conduct conversations in secret, to obtaining a sweetheart deal on a Capitol Hill condo rental from an energy lobbyist with business before his agency. Charged with leading an agency devoted to scientific inquiry and public health, Pruitt disputes the science of climate change and has rolled back or sought to impede the enforcement of many EPA rules that protect our air, land, and water from pollution by fossil fuel and chemical companies. Similar ethics issues abound for current or former Cabinet Secretaries Tom Price, Ryan Zinke, Betsy DeVos, and Ben Carson, and many others in Trump's administration.

Many folks are willing to overlook these transgressions, again, because they see that Trump is shaking up the status quo. For Democrats to have credibility, we have to be willing to hit hard at the D.C. establishment and shake things up as well. We need to do some swamp-draining of our own by pushing a strong agenda for cleaning up the system and taking money out of politics.

In addition to resisting and attacking, we also need to inspire voters, and not just assume they will turn out because they don't like Trump. We tried that in 2016, and, yeah, that didn't work out so well. If we don't start convincing people that Democrats have an identity, narrative, and agenda of their own by 2020, we are going to go into that election with big expectations and come up short just like we did in 2016, because our base will end up just as unenthusiastic about us as many of them were last time. Democrats need a bold agenda, one that's more interesting and motivating than the cautious incrementalism of too many Democratic campaigns.

What us wonky inside-the-beltway folks sometimes forget is that politics is at its heart about storytelling. Ronald Reagan was a great storyteller. Bill Clinton was a great storyteller. In 2016, the best storytellers were Bernie Sanders and Donald Trump, a shock to anyone who wasn't paying attention to the primal scream of working- and middle-class Americans for a candidate who could break the political status quo. To quote the major Democratic activist-donor Tom Steyer:

> Two people won the argument in 2016: Bernie who isn't a Democrat and Trump who is not a Republican. That was a huge statement by the American people about how much the parties are responding to the real-world issues that are facing them every single day.

We Democrats must write a narrative about our values and vision, and how we will fight to make them a reality. That story needs to have some enemies to overcome and goals that will make a substantive difference in the lives of everyday Americans. If we are not willing to clearly articulate our values, or we are too scared to fight for them, why should Americans join our team? We have to give them something to root for.

Establishing Our Own Swamp-Draining Bona Fides

Democrats are not any more trusted by most American voters than Republicans are -- voters believe we are too tied to big money interests. To change that image, we need to have our own plan to drain the swamp, and it starts with dealing with the elephant in the room: money in politics. Voters understand that Trump and the Republicans are corrupt and are not looking to drain the swamp at all, but our side just isn't trusted much either. To change that and establish more credibility with the voters, we need to be pushing the strongest possible reform message. To quote Stan Greenberg again, writing about working-class, swing voters:

> These voters... are open to an expansive Democratic economic agenda—to more benefits for child care and higher education, to tax hikes on the wealthy, to investment in infrastructure spending, and to economic policies that lead employers to boost salaries for middle- and working-class Americans, especially women. Yet they are only ready to listen when they think that Democrats understand their deeply held

belief that politics has been corrupted and government has failed. Championing reform of government and the political process is the price of admission with these voters. These white working-class and downscale voters are acutely conscious of the growing role of big money in politics and of a government that works for the 1 percent, not them.

Taking on big money in politics directly -- public financing of campaigns, reversing the Citizens United decision, ending the revolving door of special interest lobbyists in and out of government -- should be one of the very first things we talk about on the campaign trail, and one of the very first we do upon taking power in government again.

And once we really and truly drain the swamp, then we can build a home with a solid foundation.

The Foundation for the American Family's House

I have always believed in the idea of an American family. Like many families, we can be dysfunctional a lot of the time. But I think the biggest reason people responded so powerfully to Martin Luther King's "I Have a Dream" speech was the idea that Americans would one day sit down at the table of brotherhood and sisterhood and come together as a family. A unified American family is an essential part of the progressive message.

When a family works well, everyone looks out for each other; the children are given everything they need to grow up safe and strong; and adults flourish as they settle in to middle and old age. Right now, the American family is in bad shape. Selfishness rules the day; everyone is fighting. The house we used to live in together has burned down. What Democrats need to do is to rebuild the house and bring everyone back together. So what I want to do first is build a foundation for our rebuilt home.

I'm not going to do what is so often done in Democratic politics, which is to carefully check off a very long list of wonky issues. If that's what you are hungering for, you bought the wrong book. For that I recommend you look up Hillary Clinton's policy papers or the 2016 Democratic platform. While I certainly don't agree with everything on either list, most Democrats agree there's a lot of good stuff there. In fact, the platform was widely (and accurately) lauded as the most progressive in the party's history, while having almost nothing in it that would have been politically unpopular.

What I want to do here instead is build a foundation for a house in which we can live together comfortably, and then lay out enough of an agenda for a good Democratic candidate to run on. My foundation is made up of four bedrock ideas that reinforce each other:

1. **Democrats are focused on helping working families by fighting greedy and powerful special interests that dominate our economy and democracy.** Old-school populism still does work, as candidates from Trump to Bernie Sanders have shown, so long as it is combined with a "clean up D.C. corruption" message. This basic concept covers a lot of ground: raising wages and benefits; getting workers a better retirement; strengthening unions; fighting Wall Street, Big Pharma, and Big Oil, and other big money special interests; enacting tougher anti-trust laws and progressive taxes; helping small businesses compete with big businesses and family farmers compete with corporate agriculture; and many other economic issues. The progressive populist agenda provides Democrats with a strong contrast between our identity and the Republican identity. Drawing this contrast is critical, so that voters can discern a difference between parties and between candidates.

2. **Democrats are committed to fairness and justice as the cornerstones of a decent society.** Our party must govern by a basic rule: we cannot allow the powerful to prey on those with less power. Simple idea, transformative when you put it in practice. Greedy corporations with insider connections shouldn't be able to play by a different set of rules from their competitors. Cough, cough, Goldman Sachs. Huge monopolistic conglomerates shouldn't be able to keep honest, hardworking business people from making a living and expect taxpayers to pick up the tab to boot. Cough, cough, Wal-Mart. Employees should never be fired for trying to organize a union, and they shouldn't have to pay a higher rate of taxes than their wealthy CEO. Bosses should not be allowed to sexually harass employees. Whether they have committed a

crime or not, people with black or brown skin should not have to live in fear of being shot by the police. Workers should receive equal pay for equal work, and not face discrimination for their identity.

Fairness and decency also extend to our foreign policy. People in poor countries around the world don't hate us because we have freedom, as the Republican Party likes to say. They hate us because they think that we exploit them for their natural resources and help to keep corrupt politicians in power for our own benefit, that we are more likely to bomb them than help them. We should have a strong enough military to defend our borders and keep us as safe as possible from terrorism, but we don't want to be bombing first and asking questions later. Being free and strong means having the confidence to build more alliances with other free people, and going to war only as a last resort, not as the first.

These things are just common sense decency and fairness, and the Democratic Party should not only never shy away from them, but be proud of embracing them. A basic sense of fairness should be part of our party's core identity.

3. **Democrats are the party of building the future.** Trump wants to return to a mythical golden age. "Make America great again" harkens back to the '50s era when men had power over women, wealthy white guys ran the show, and America ran the world. But if you weren't wealthy and white and male, your life wasn't so great. Democrats believe in a world where wrongs are actually righted, where women and people of color are recognized as equal. And we believe in creating a future by investing in tomorrow: in education and infrastructure; in green energy instead of the fossil fuels that are disrupting the climate; in research and development so that the jobs, technologies, and medicines of tomorrow are built.

4. **Democrats want you to be free to pursue your dreams.** Republicans want to give more money to the wealthy, ostensibly because they believe in the free-market fallacy of

trickle-down economics, and that only the wealthy understand how to create jobs. Democrats know that businesses only succeed, and jobs only get created, through consumer demand and government investment.

But the biggest demand, and thus the biggest job creation, comes from a strong and growing middle class, wherein people have enough money to raise their families, buy products and services, and even take some risks like starting a new business. If all Americans are given the freedom to make a successful life for themselves, then the economy will get stronger for all of us. People should have the freedom to control their own destinies: if and when to start a family, if and when to change jobs, if and when to buy a house or start a business. If people have these freedoms and the support they need to achieve their dreams, America will be a great place to live.

Ten Big Ideas for the 21st Century

The four principles listed above tell people the story of what we believe, the foundation upon which we must build. The issues I outline below add structure to Our American House. There are many incredibly important issues, and a book on policy or a candidate's party's platform should go into those issues in-depth. But when we are trying to win elections, we should keep it simple.

Does that mean our candidates should not have a well-honed, comprehensive issue agenda? Absolutely not. Our American House needs more than those four foundation cornerstones. It needs some rooms built into it and some furniture in those rooms. Voters do care about what you are planning to do for them, as do the activists and online contributors we need to reach, and candidates should lay out an agenda in a big, bold way.

To reiterate, I'm not a fan of long and exhaustive laundry lists, delineating every conceivable issue. However, I am a big believer in the power of ten. Moses covered a lot of ground with those Ten Commandments; had some big ideas with lots of nuance and depth; but he still kept it to ten. (I'm not comparing myself to Moses by the way!) And there's something about the number that resonates, which is why Newt Gingrich's 'Contract with America' had ten points to it, and Dave Letterman had his Top 10 lists. (Nor am I comparing myself to Letterman or Newt, the latter of which especially should comfort you.)

So here are my 10 Big Issues, which flow from the working families, fairness, future, and freedom foundation above:

1. **Get big money out of politics and reduce the influence of monopolistic big businesses on the markets.** We have to make small businesses, consumers, and workers more powerful by breaking up the mega-corporations that distort the American political system and marketplace. If you've been paying attention, you probably guessed this would be toward the top of my top 10 list. Whether the sector is banking, tech, retail, food, airlines or anything else, any corporation big enough to distort the marketplace so much that they can destroy their competitors and abuse workers and consumers needs to be taken down several notches. If an airline can physically drag a man with a legitimate ticket off the plane after he has boarded and not lose market share because there are so few airlines, something is desperately wrong. Anti-trust enforcement needs to become a real thing again and, as noted above, every agency in government needs to be examining how it can foster more open competition through its regulatory and procurement process.

    When companies get to be the size of Amazon, Exxon, Facebook, Google, J.P. Morgan Chase, United, and Wal-Mart, they have too much power. Too much market power, and with that kind of money, too much political power. Citizens United, the Supreme Court decision that allows corporations to spend unlimited money on elections, must be overturned. We also need public financing of campaigns, so that more diverse candidates can run and not rely on big money donors. Politicians shouldn't be able to take money from mega-corporations who contract with the government or have business in front of the committees which have jurisdiction over their activities.

2. **End all carbon emissions by at least 2050.** This can be done and must be done, and ideally at a much sooner date.

My good friend in the Senate, Jeff Merkley, has a bill to accomplish the transition off fossil fuels by 2050, and in the House, Tulsi Gabbard followed Jeff's lead with a proposal to do so by 2035. And I've even gotten into the legislative game – my advocacy nonprofit, American Family Voices, has teamed up with "Climate Cowboy" Dave Freeman (one of the key people who first created the EPA) to push these bills to drop the false solution of cap-and-trade and to require faster mandates. As Dave likes to say, "The house is on fire now. Mother Nature doesn't care about all the cap-and-trade bullshit. We must mandate renewables."

This transition will not only dramatically reduce climate change; it will create tens of millions of jobs. The focus should not just be on electricity generation, which is the focus of a number existing legislative proposals. The transition needs to include transportation, infrastructure, architecture, and agriculture as well. The technology is already there to get this done; there are new tech innovations in clean energy all the time; and the costs continue to drop.

The markets are already moving in this direction as well, as solar and wind are becoming cheaper and green energy investments are becoming profitable. But we need our country to accelerate the transition. We need to phase out and eventually ban carbon energy, but in the meantime we need a sizable carbon tax; we also need serious investments in and tax breaks for clean energy. We need to work with farmers to move them away from fossil fuel intensive operations. We need to require car companies to manufacture 100% electric cars.

To be enough to make a difference in corporate behavior, the carbon tax needs to be pretty significant. Part of the money from the carbon tax should go into a fund for workers currently working in the fossil fuels industry, so that they have a lengthy transition to find good new jobs (maybe in the green energy business). Part of it should go into low-income areas to help them make the energy transition, and part should go to consumers in the form of a dividend to help pay the increased cost of energy from the tax.

3. **Ensure that Americans have access to affordable health care.** A clear majority of Americans agree that we need universal health care coverage, like every other industrialized nation in the world. The most efficient way to get there is Medicare For All, which I strongly support. However, many of us who have been working on health care in-depth for a long time worry that it will be very tough to ask those Americans in love with their health care plan to give it up. (I was an early adviser to Hillary on getting her health care plan passed in 1993; helped write the plan for passing the Affordable Care Act in 2008; and was part of the team that worked to defeat the ACA repeal in 2017.) An alternative idea, created by the same Jacob Hacker who came up with the idea for a public option, would allow anyone of any age not covered by a good plan to sign up for Medicare, essentially Medicare for All Who Want It. This idea would have some inefficiencies that are not in Medicare For All, but might be a good next step. Either plan would be a vast improvement in our current health care system.

Health care for all, incidentally, means full health care services for women as well as men. Radical, I know. But women should have easy access to family planning and reproductive health services -- and yes, that includes poor women: the infamous Hyde Amendment has to go.

4. **Reform our criminal justice system, and decriminalize drug addiction and marijuana.** Our society has created so much waste - of people, tax dollars, and opportunities - by keeping so many of our citizens in prisons and jails. The hyper get-tough-on-crime wave fostered by both political parties in the 1980s and '90s was a terrible mistake. Not only would justice be better served, but our economy would be stronger and more productive if far fewer people were locked up on petty charges, and instead received a decent education and opportunities for living-wage jobs.

Furthermore, our decades-long War on Drugs has been an abject failure, and disproportionately waged against black and brown people. Just look at the disparity in sentences between cocaine and crack, the former used disproportionately by white people and the latter by black folks. There is no justifiable reason for this disparity – it's racism plain and simple, and it has irreparably harmed generations of black communities.

We're in the middle of an opioid crisis, where thousands are dying from overdoses, driven by the easy flow of addictive painkillers from Big Pharma to the public. Addicts should not be in jail; they should be in rehab. We must hold big pharmaceutical companies and their doctor-dealers accountable for getting their patients hooked on these deadly pills.

You know what's not deadly? Pot. There's not ever been a single reported death of a marijuana overdose. There is no reason that pot smokers should be in prison. We should make pot legal, and release the people currently in prison for using it. That way, we can regulate it and tax it, as is being done in more and more states across the country from California to Colorado to right here in the District of Columbia. It's the other booming green industry, and Democrats should harness it. Kudos to Sen. Cory Booker and Rep. Barbara Lee for leading the way with comprehensive marijuana reform in 2017, and to Sen. Chuck Schumer for recently committing to introduce legislation to decriminalize marijuana federally.

5. **Fix the country's immigration system.** The whole immigration debate in America has been ridiculous since long before Trump was president, although he has certainly made it far more blatantly racist. But there's been a generally agreed upon framework for a comprehensive immigration deal for a long damn time. It has as its centerpiece a reasonable path to citizenship. Let's stop messing around and get this done. If we do, pretty much everyone except hard core racists will breathe a big sigh of relief that this long

nightmarish debate is finally over: comprehensive immigration reform with a clear path to citizenship has been supported by a large majority of the American people for a decade.

6. **Build a great system of public education from pre-school through college.** Rather than privatize education like Trump's Secretary of Education, Betsy DeVos, wants to do, we need a stronger public education for all our children. Well-paid and well-trained teachers, universal broadband fiber, and buildings that aren't falling apart are obvious components for such an educational system, but those things are lacking in a great many schools.

Public college education should also be free or damn close to it. Anyone who wants to go to college should be able to do so. When Abraham Lincoln and a vastly different kind of Republican Party set up land-grant universities, the idea was to have a system of affordable public schools for poor and middle-income people. Now tuition costs and the escalating cost of student debt have made going to college all but impossible for many middle- and working-class students. For those who do graduate, many can't find jobs in the field of their choosing, and are locked into jobs they don't like just so they can pay off enormous student debt.

7. **Create a National Infrastructure Bank to finally make the investments we need in our nation's infrastructure.** Economists say we have more than a three trillion-dollar gap in the funds needed for roads, highways, bridges, airports, electric grid improvements, school buildings, and other kinds of physical infrastructure. I don't believe even a Democratic Congress would ever fund that much spending, but Congresswoman Rosa DeLauro and my good friend, New York businessman Leo Hindery, have come up with a plan that will provide much more of the funding needed: a National Infrastructure Bank. Leo has had a lot of conversations with public pension fund managers around the country, and many of them would make investments in this bank if it was backed up by a federal guarantee. This kind of

proposal would help fund the repairs and new buildings the nation needs, and would create millions of good-paying jobs at the same time.

8. **Invest in communities that need jobs and economic development the most.** Democrats haven't always been willing to talk about how new job creation should be partly targeted to the places that need it the most. Really, this is just common sense. Most of what I have been describing is going to generate jobs and economic activity broadly, but sometimes communities that are especially trapped in poverty get left behind. Poor neighborhoods in inner cities and inner-ring suburbs, American Indian reservations, and much of rural America have been stuck in a cycle of poverty, or at least stagnancy, for a long time, and will need some targeted investment to get them jumpstarted.

9. **Empower working people again.** You didn't think this old labor guy was going to leave this one out, did you? But this isn't just about unions: workers in general, whether in a union or not, need to have more power in relation to their employers. Yes, working people need to have the laws restructured, so that it is easier to organize a union if they want to do so, but they also need to not be at the whim of employers constantly changing their work hours on part-time jobs. They need paid time off when a new baby comes into the family or when someone gets sick, and employer assistance with decent day care. They need to make a living wage of at least $15 an hour, so that if they work full-time they don't live in poverty, and that includes waitresses and waiters who shouldn't have rely on tips to survive. Women shouldn't have to sign a Non-Disclosure Agreement that keeps them from telling people they have been sexually harassed, and LGBT folks shouldn't ever be discriminated against. Right now, employers have so much power that they can abuse workers in so many ways it makes your head spin. It's time to change this power dynamic.

Ultimately, this country should be guaranteeing a job to everyone who wants to work. I believe that the kind of economic policies I advocate will create enough jobs and income for working people that we will be at full employment, and that if we build the same kind of vibrant, growing middle class we had in the middle of the last century, it will be a self-reinforcing cycle. But with technology taking a lot of jobs away, and the ups and downs of economic cycles, the government should also make sure that everyone who wants a job gets a decent-paying job.

In its May 2017 report "Toward a New Marshall Plan for America," the Center for American Progress proposed a federal jobs guarantee. Here's what their experts think it will cost:

> Such an expanded public employment program could, for example, have a target of maintaining the employment rate for prime-age workers without a bachelor's degree at the 2000 level of 79 percent. Currently, this would require the creation of 4.4 million jobs. At a living wage—which we can approximate as $15 per hour plus the cost of contributions to Social Security and Medicare via payroll taxes—the direct cost of each job would be approximately $36,000 annually. Thus, a rough estimate of the costs of this employment program would be about $158 billion in the current year. This is approximately one-quarter of Trump's proposed tax cut for the wealthy on an annual basis.

In April of 2018, Senator Cory Booker, a major contender for the Democratic presidential nomination in 2020, announced that he will introduce a bill to guarantee jobs in a three-year pilot program in up to 15 high-unemployment communities across the country. His cosponsors? Several of the other major presidential contenders: Bernie Sanders, who is drafting his own competing bill, Elizabeth Warren, Kirsten Gillibrand, Kamala Harris, and Jeff Merkley. Along with other recent proposals like Medicare for All, legalizing marijuana, and creating a postal banking system, we may well have a presidential progressive arms race on our hands! Which is the way it should be.

10. **Enact a new budget and tax system that is fair to working people.** The outrageous Republican tax scam gave 83% of the benefits to the top 1%. On top of the loophole-ridden and already too regressive tax system coming from way too many years of Republican control of Congress, we now have a tax system that is both radically unfair and highly inadequate to fund government services.

Some of that money can come from the enormous waste in the federal budget. Yes, the Republicans are right that there is waste. But they are dead wrong on what it is. Republicans think the waste is Social Security, Medicare, Medicaid, and education – the programs that actually help people. The reality is that the military budget, which just grew by an additional $80 billion a year, is bloated beyond belief and could be cut by $200 billion a year without lowering the number or pay of our soldiers or changing our preparedness level one iota. Big agribusiness companies are given multi-billion-dollar subsidies that they don't need to be profitable. Government contracting reform, particularly refusing to pay for cost over-runs or delayed delivery of services the way the private sector does, would save us at least $100 billion dollars a year. The 30-year-plus trend toward privatizing government services, instead of saving money, has been another source of wasted tax dollars. I could go on, but I'll spare you the exhaustive laundry list.

Restoring the progressivity in our tax system and taxing economic activities we want to discourage are going to be the main places we look for dollars. One example of the latter I've already mentioned is a carbon tax. Another policy idea is a tiny tax on speculative trading on Wall Street that could raise hundreds of billions of dollars over a decade. Another is closing the carried interest loophole, an idea that even Donald Trump campaigned for. (But Wall Streeters love it, so color me shocked that it remains in place.) We need to fully reinstate the estate tax: rich kids shouldn't inherit everything tax-free. The most often cited reason for eliminating the estate tax is the breakup of family farms, but family farmers can already set up trusts that allow them to avoid farm asset liquidation.

Most of all, we just need the millionaires and billionaires to pay their fair share of taxes. History indicates that doing this won't hurt us at all, contrary to conservative orthodoxy. The last two times we raised taxes on the wealthy, in 1993 and during the Obama years, the economy performed well. So well that during the Clinton years, we ran a budget surplus. When taxes were at their highest level on the wealthy in the 1940s, '50s, and '60s, the economy was the strongest we've ever seen. We can do this again, and invest that extra money into better jobs and infrastructure to build a stronger economy. Everyone wins in the long run. (Although the Koch brothers will whine a lot.)

A Sturdy House for the Future

Now that we have the foundation and the primary issues for our agenda, what's next?

An agenda is a good start, but it's not enough. What we need to do next is tell the American people who we are, where we came from, and how we will fight for them. The American people need to hear this story because we have lost our way in recent years, and who we are is a bit of a mystery to many voters.

We also need to engage the Republicans in the battle of ideas over the most basic iconic concepts in American culture. My final chapters are about how to show Americans what we believe in and who we are as Democrats.

CHAPTER SEVEN: THE DEFINITIONAL FIGHT OVER FREEDOM

In the great challenge of the next few years, when our democratic society is at a crossroads unprecedented in our nation's history, we must reclaim our courage and identity as a party. We can best do this by having definitional fights over issues, but also over ideas, which matter far more than the cynics and technocrats think they do. Big definitional issue fights, like the ones we had in 2017 over health care and taxes, matter a lot. But big idea battles matter too. Central to our winning the message wars with a demagogue like Trump is winning the battle over how freedom is defined.

When you ask people what America means to them, what word best defines our country, the word is freedom. And the Republicans have wrapped themselves in that word even more than they wrap themselves in the flag.

Let me blunt here, and a little vulgar. For Donald Trump and the Republican Party now thoroughly remade in his image, freedom is solely defined as this: the freedom to be an asshole. There honestly is no better way to describe it.

Trump and the rich white men who run the Republican Party yell loudly at every turn that they believe in freedom. What they want is the freedom to do whatever they want, whenever they want, to whomever they want. Period. They want the freedom to pay the lowest possible wages and benefits to their workers. They want the freedom to avoid paying taxes to support the roads, water system, police, education, and military forces that keep them safe and benefit them. They want the freedom to discriminate against any group of people they dislike and then abuse the people they do hire. They want the freedom to pollute the air and water no matter the costs for other people or future generations. They want the freedom to crush their competitors and cheat their customers and even crash the economy without any consequences at all.

Our Koch Problem

Over the last three decades, the people who have most shaped the Republican definition of freedom are Charles and David Koch. The libertarian oil billionaire Koch brothers have hosted many secret conferences with other conservative billionaires and mega-millionaires. My colleague, and one of the editors of this book, Lauren Windsor, produces a grassroots reporting web-show called The Undercurrent. In 2014, she published several hours of audio from a source who was at one of these donor retreats. This individual had taped many of the speeches and sessions, which featured Republican stars like Senators Mitch McConnell and Marco Rubio, House Freedom Caucus leader Jim Jordan, and a variety of other candidates.

Much of what the Republican politicians said was appalling. Mitch McConnell, for example, said that the worst day of his political life was when McCain-Feingold was passed, legislation regulating money in politics. Mind you McConnell had then been in office for 30 years, during the September 11 attacks, the Iraq War, and the 2008 financial meltdown – but it was campaign finance disclosures that were the worst! Just to give you an indication of the now-Senate Majority Leader's indebtedness to the tycoons (at the time he was the Minority Leader), he told the Kochs that he didn't "know where we [the Republicans] would be without you."

But the truly scary speakers were Charles Koch himself and his minions. In a series of big ideological speeches given the first day of their retreat, which McConnell called "very inspiring," Charles Koch, his "grand strategist" Richard Fink, and the Charles Koch Institute's VP for Research and Policy, Will Ruger, laid out a vision of government and society that would be pretty terrifying to anyone this side of Ayn Rand. The minimum wage, which Fink said leads to Nazism, should be abolished. Homeless people should be told to "get off [their] ass and work hard like we did." Government should get out of the business of anything except the police force, military, and judicial system — no Social Security, Medicare, Medicaid, public education, student loans, clean air or water protections, national or state parks, food safety, or Wall Street oversight.

This extreme right-wing agenda has become the Republican definition of freedom: let us do whatever we want and the devil take the hindmost. Anyone who doesn't get rich only has themselves to blame. No one deserves help of any kind from the government or anyone else.

The Democrats' Definition of Freedom

Democrats have a different definition of freedom. As the party of the people, we have a heritage and legacy of freedom. The founders of our party wrote the Declaration of Independence and the Bill of Rights. We championed FDR's Four Freedoms -- freedom of speech, freedom of religion, freedom from want, and freedom from fear. And we helped the Civil Rights movement free African-Americans from the violence of Jim Crow. But today, when democracy and the very meaning of freedom is on the line, we don't spend nearly enough time talking about freedom. Most importantly, we don't spend enough time directly contesting the Republicans on their definition of the word.

What Democrats are for, what we need to fight for, is the freedom of regular people to build a better future for themselves and their families. Americans have certain freedoms enshrined in the Bill of Rights, but in many areas of their lives, they don't feel free. You don't have freedom if you haven't had a raise in ten years, while the cost of your health care and groceries have skyrocketed and you are being squeezed to death. You don't have freedom if you need to work three different part-time, minimum-wage jobs in order to feed your kids and keep a roof over their heads. You don't have freedom if you have to fly home to take care of your elderly mom who just got sick and desperately needs you, and there's only one available flight with an airline that charges you an outrageous amount of money and then squeezes you into a horribly uncomfortable seat. You don't have freedom if you are a small farmer and there's only one chicken company who will buy your chickens and they will only pay a rock bottom price. You don't have freedom if people with AR-15s come into your school and start shooting whomever they see. You don't have freedom if lead-laced tap water is poisoning your kids, and your state is slow-walking the clean-up effort. And you certainly don't have freedom if you are a kid and your parents are being ripped apart from you in a deportation raid.

Most Americans aren't looking for the freedom to be assholes. They are looking for the freedom to work at a job they like where they will be treated with dignity. They want to make enough money to raise their kids in a decent house in a decent neighborhood and send them to a safe school. They want to retire with some basic economic security. They want to build a solid, stable life for themselves and their families. That's the freedom that matters to them. If they own a business, they want the freedom to innovate and create products they are proud of, and to build their business without unfair competition. They want to be able to be good to their workers and their community while still making a good living. They want a level playing field.

With Donald Trump in the White House and his band of marauding Republicans following in his wake, this battle over which kind of freedom we are looking for in America is the defining battle of our times. Especially if we want to be the party of the people again. The central question isn't whether government is good or bad, or too big or too small. The question is whether government is fighting for the freedom to screw workers, or whether it is fighting for the freedom of workers not to be exploited by unscrupulous employers. Is the government giving Wells Fargo the freedom to rip customers off, or is it giving customers the freedom from being cheated? Is government granting Exxon the freedom to pollute the air and water, or is it giving all of us the freedom of breathing clean air and drinking clean water?

When our government is run by people who are looting the Treasury to serve their own greed, the question about the nature of freedom is at the heart of our political debate. Never forget the Republican ideal, so bluntly put forth by GOP anti-tax icon Grover Norquist: "I don't want to abolish government. I simply want to reduce it to the size where I can drag it into the bathroom and drown it in the bathtub." This is a statement of obscene privilege. The government provides many essential services that millions of Americans depend on, services that Congressional Republicans are doing their best to eliminate, services I've already enumerated. Democrats need to show working people we will fight for them and against a marauding class that believes in "socialism for me, but not for thee."

Lauren calls this idea of freedom 'progressive libertarianism': we don't want government getting into our private lives unnecessarily, but if we want to attain the highest degree of individual liberty possible for the most people possible, we sure as hell need government to act as a buffer against corporate power run amok. Without it, the only people who are truly free are rich people, and the rest of us are wage slaves. Progressive libertarianism is the right kind of balance for the Democratic Party to strike.

The Freedom to Live in Peace

As I write this, it appears that Trump is assembling a war cabinet, a group of people whose entire careers have been distinguished by hyper-aggressiveness for supporting military intervention. The worst of these is John Bolton, his new National Security Advisor, who has often been described as "a hawk among hawks" in the Bush administration. In classic Trump fashion, he appointed a man to run White House intel operations who is well-known for manipulating intelligence data to get us into the Iraq War.

There is nothing more costly and destabilizing than war. The Iraq War cost trillions of dollars; killed and maimed hundreds of thousands of Americans and Iraqis; and destabilized the entire Middle East region for the foreseeable future. War with Iran, which is far stronger than Iraq under Hussein – or North Korea, which has nuclear weapons – is almost certain to be much costlier in terms of both lives and treasure.

When our leaders go to war, they always say that "we are fighting for our freedom." But what kind of freedom? Is it the freedom to exploit the other country's resources? Is it the freedom to impose our will upon others, whatever the consequences?

War is always evil. Sometimes it is necessary, as I believe World War II was, but even then, it is a choice a country should make only as the absolute last resort, the least bad of a lot of bad options. Trump and Bolton appear to want to go to war as the first resort, to satisfy their desire for macho domination.

It is urgently important that Democrats oppose this administration when it embarks on another foolhardy war. The last time this country officially went to war, too many Democrats in Congress -- including House Leader Dick Gephardt, Senate Majority Leader Tom Daschle, and the most prominent Democrat then in Congress, Senator Hillary Clinton -- voted to allow Bush to invade Iraq. Gephardt's Chief of Staff told me before the vote that Democratic support for the war resolution was a good political move for the upcoming 2002 elections because "it would take the war off the table as an issue and allow Democrats to focus on the economy." But it was a terrible political move even short term, as the vast majority of Democrats across the country opposed the war and having the party leaders in Congress support it depressed base voter turnout, resulting in a good Republican year that cost us control of the Senate and several House seats.

The long-term politics were even worse. Bush and his Dark Sith Lord Dick Cheney had lied about Saddam Hussein having weapons of mass destruction and the Iraq War became a terrible debacle. Democrats who voted for it were haunted by the vote for years to come. Gephardt's presidential bid in 2004 died a quick death in Iowa, a state he won the first time he ran for president; Daschle lost his 2004 Senate re-election bid; Bush beat John Kerry in the 2004 general election, with Kerry's waffling on why he supported the war being a major factor. But Hillary Clinton was perhaps the hardest hit. She lost to Barack Obama in the 2008 primary, with her support for the war and Obama's early opposition being one of the biggest factors, and then she lost again to Trump in 2016, with her image as a war hawk being a major factor for many Bernie backers whose support she failed to win in the general election.

Democrats would do well to remember this political history. Wars occasionally provide a short-term political boost for the presidents that start them, but rarely do they help them over the long run. The last president who got us into or escalated a major war and was still popular at the end of their presidency was FDR.

The next war will be worse under Donald Trump. This Commander-in-Chief will blunder into it without thought or preparation, and then constantly be saying dumb things that will undermine (or even give away) our own strategy. And it will be worse for any Democrats who support it because the Democratic voter opposition to a war coming from Trump will have far more intensity and depth than the reaction to the Iraq War. I am also convinced that Trump will not benefit from the immediate sugar high most presidents get as they go into war because the 55% of voters who have solidly opposed him from Day One will be highly cynical about any conflict he starts. He has very little credibility with the majority of the American people.

If Trump takes us to war, it will be a defining moment for his presidency, but also for the Democratic Party. Let's hope our leadership meets the test.

Freedom and Fairness

An essential measure of freedom is that people do not feel the weight of oppression in their daily lives. To make the most obvious of points, slaves were not free. Every day, from the moment they woke up until the time they went to sleep, they knew they were not free. But people living in the Jim Crow South knew they were not free either. Indigenous peoples forced to live on Indian reservations knew they were not free. And people who live in grinding poverty or are trapped in debt anywhere know they are not free. People of color, who are far more likely to be stopped and arrested by police, far more likely to be shot by police, far more likely to be convicted of crimes, do not feel free. Undocumented immigrants living in daily fear of ICE raids do not feel free. People in the LGBT community who are discriminated against do not feel free.

Democrats should be very clear that issues derided by conservatives and some centrists as "identity politics" are really about freedom and fairness. We do not want to live in a society where bigotry flourishes, where poor folks and communities of color enjoy fewer freedoms than rich white people. As I wrote earlier, most voters will not have a problem with us speaking out against bigotry, so long as it is not the only issue we mention or seem to care about in our speeches and campaign content.

Talking about the ideas of freedom and fairness side by side, and bringing an economic analysis to these issues should be a critical piece of our communications strategy.

Freedom as a Cornerstone

Americans see freedom as a cornerstone of our society. In a recent survey, registered voters were asked, "Which of two or three of the following words best describes what it means to be an American?" They were given a list of words including freedom, opportunity, equality, patriotism, melting pot, justice, strength, fairness, innovation, courage, bravery, industry, unique. "Freedom" received 61 percent. No other word even came close.

Our political language should focus on the idea of freedom as intrinsic to everything Democrats stand for and believe in. Republicans have always argued that because they are for less government (in theory, at least -- government always seems to grow on the GOP's watch, just in the wrong ways), that means they are for more freedom, because government shouldn't be able to tell people what to do.

In fact, while government does sometimes need to play a restrictive role in terms of harmful activity (don't kill people, don't rob people, don't run a red light, don't dump poison in the river), only a small percentage of what government actually does is telling people what they can't do. Most of what government does involves protecting people (military, police, firefighters, food and drug safety, making sure our air and water are clean and our kids' toys are safe); serving people in various ways (libraries, the Department of Motor Vehicles, the National Park Service); empowering people (education, job training, the Consumer Financial Protection Bureau); or distributing money, health care, and food (Social Security, student loans, Medicare, Medicaid, disaster relief, Head Start, food stamps). Not only does all that not take away our freedom, I would argue that such things foster more freedom and allow us more dignity, a la Maslow's hierarchy of needs.

We should press our case for our definition of freedom with vigor. The Declaration of Independence started out by saying that all of us are created equal, and that we were endowed by our creator with life, liberty, and the pursuit of happiness. The two greatest, most influential speeches in American history ended with an ode to freedom: Lincoln's Gettysburg Address ("…that this nation under God shall have a new birth of freedom…"), and MLK's "I Have a Dream" speech ("free at last, free at last, thank God almighty we are free at last"). Freedom is our nation's iconic hope, at the center of what it means to be an American. This definitional fight over Trump's kind of freedom versus our kind of freedom will be central to deciding our nation's fate.

CHAPTER EIGHT: THE PARTY OF THE PEOPLE

People can point to lots of mistakes as to why Democrats have lost so many elections in the last ten years, and I have talked about many of them in this book. But most fundamental of all is simply that we have lost our way in recent years. We have gone from being the party of the boldness of FDR, the party of the courage and eloquence of Martin Luther King and the Kennedys, to being the party that wavers in holding Wall Street accountable, the party that runs away from its own accomplishments on health care, the party that repeatedly pushes immigration reform to the backburner.

If the defining characteristics of Republicans in the last quarter century are that they have overreached and gotten ever more extreme and uncompromising, the defining traits of Democrats are, even when they have had power, that they have become more cautious and fearful of doing too much and being too bold. For the former, see Mitch McConnell re Obama's Supreme Court nominee Merrick Garland, and for the latter, Obama dropping the public option from the health care debate. (Thankfully, because of Bernie's strong showing in 2016 and Elizabeth Warren's popularity, this is beginning to change under the Trump administration, with the progressive arms race now underway between the Democratic presidential contenders.) There have been some sterling exceptions to this trend: Bill Clinton standing strong against Gingrich in the 1995 budget wars; Teddy Kennedy brilliantly out-maneuvering Dole and Gingrich to win an increase in the minimum wage and the CHIP program; Obama, Pelosi, and Reid dragging health care reform across the finish line, and standing up to the Wall Street lobby to win the Consumer Financial Protection Bureau.

I've been incredibly proud recently that Democrats in Congress voted 100% against the repeal of the ACA and the deeply regressive Republican tax plan, both signs that maybe, just maybe, our party is starting to get our mojo back. But too many Democrats, too much of the time in the last couple of decades, have seemed like they are adrift at sea, unsure of their moorings. Afraid of alienating anyone and convinced against all experience that some Republicans are open to compromise, Democrats often have tried to be too many things to too many constituencies. That lack of principle isn't exactly stirring. What Republicans understand is that they are unlikely to persuade Democrats to vote for their legislative priorities, and so they play hardball from the outset. Many voters tend to be more drawn to the passion of the Republicans than to the caution of Democrats, even if they have thought the Republicans were a little cracked.

To find our passion -- and spines -- again, Democrats need to remember our history and get back to our roots.

Rediscovering Our Roots

The Democratic Party was founded in the earliest days of our nation in the 1790s by Thomas Jefferson and James Madison. To say that these founding fathers were far from perfect and were hypocritical in their love of freedom while owning slaves understates the matter: they knew that slavery was evil and still chose to benefit from it. We should never forget or forgive those sins. Democrats who love our country and party need to come to terms with that stain upon our history.

And yet it is still worth reclaiming the ideas the party was founded on, to remember the early ideological battles and lineage from which we spring. Steeped in hypocrisy that our founders were, they still embraced important ideas: equality, community, pluralism, and democracy.

The Democratic Party quite literally began in a fight over whether Wall Street bankers, or farmers and workers, should control the economy. In the early decisions about structuring our new country's debts, Treasury Secretary Alexander Hamilton (who wasn't nearly as good a fellow as the musical made him out to be) gave all the benefits to his New York banker friends on Wall Street, screwing famers and workers in the process. Jefferson and Monroe were outraged and fought back. When George Washington retired as president and John Adams ran to continue Washington's and Hamilton's policies, Jefferson mounted a challenge that almost succeeded. Four years later, he tried again and won, kicking off a 24-year period of Democrats running the government.

That the government should be of, by, and for the people has always been a foundational principle of the Democratic Party. Hamilton, on the other hand, wanted the government to enter into a permanent partnership with big New York banks to run the economy. According to some historical sources, at a dinner party he told a Democrat advocating for the people that "your people are a great beast." The other leading Federalist, John Adams, feared the idea of expanding the vote to non-property owners because someday people might want to expand the vote to "even women and slaves."

By contrast, the founders of the Democratic Party wanted the big banks to have less power and working people to have more power. They wanted to expand democracy, so that the government would be more responsive to everyday working people. The name "Democratic" Party represented that idea and identity. They were literally pro-democracy and in favor of the people governing. Democrats from the very beginning fought for more, rather than fewer, people getting the right to vote; more people getting a good public education; and more power for small businesses, farmers and workers (outside of the slaves they sadly left behind) instead of more power for wealthy elites.

This is why, for more than 200 years, the Democratic Party was widely known as the party of the people. That's what Jefferson and Madison were proud to call it; the same for William Jennings Bryan 100 hundred years later; and FDR 50 years after that. It's what JFK and LBJ called it, too. Being the party of the people is a part of our DNA.

But we have drifted from this identity. Bill Clinton's political and fundraising success as a "pro-business" Democrat - more pro-big business than pro-small business as I described in Chapter 5 - was a part of the shift. The decline of labor membership, which has for a century helped anchor the party in the working class, was another factor. Most of all, getting hooked on a steady diet of Big

Money contributions has made Democrats nervous at bucking the powers that be in Wall Street, Silicon Valley, and the other centers of big business power.

But without our identity as the party of the people, the party of regular working folks, what is our identity? Without our history as the heirs of Jefferson, FDR, King, and the Kennedys, who are we?

We haven't had a good answer. And so, we have found ourselves drifting. I have reviewed a lot of research on the question of the Democratic Party's brand with American voters, and I can tell you for a fact that it is mush. Voters in focus groups and surveys can't tell you what Democrats stand for, or what they would fight for. Voters aren't sure if Democrats are coastal elites, the party of Hollywood, pro-labor people, environmentalists, immigrants and Black Lives Matter activists, or wonky D.C. insiders. Large majorities of the public sure know what Trump and the Republicans are all about, and they don't like it, but the Democrats? No idea.

Voters aren't sure because we Democrats aren't sure. I have been in countless conversations over the last 20 years where someone has said, "We need to do a better job of telling our story, describing the Democratic Party, and/or telling people what we stand for." But we never seem to settle on a brand, a story, or an agenda because we are riven by disparate factions with different and at times competing agendas, making the unification process akin to herding cats.

Picking Definitional Fights

There are so many fights we must rally to in the Trump presidency. I describe it to people as the Hundred-Front War, and sometimes I think that is an understatement. We are in a constant state of threat from the White House and Congressional Republicans on health care, the environment, war-mongering, labor rights, civil rights and civil liberties, rolling back good regulations... The list goes on and on, with new challenges every single week.

In these times, more than ever, Democrats need to define ourselves as the party of the people. We need to show people that we are fighting for them. Where we govern, we need to deliver. Innovative and progressive mayors like Bill de Blasio from NYC,

Nan Whaley from Dayton, Chris Beutler from my old home town of Lincoln, Eric Garcetti from LA, and Marty Walsh from Boston have been doing this, as have Democrats in California and other states where they have the reins of power. And when we are the party of opposition, as we are in the federal government and many states, we need to pick some fights on big issues that matter in everyone's lives.

In the last chapter, I talked about the definitional fight over the idea of freedom and its importance to winning in the long run. However, on a more down-to-earth level, we also need to have definitional fights over the central issues of the day. We have just done battle on two of the big ones: health care and taxes. We won both of those fights from a messaging perspective. Polling was clear that while those legislative battles were going on, voters agreed with the way we were talking about the legislation far more than they agreed with the Republicans. If you have any doubt, all you have to do is note that even the Democrats from some of the reddest states in America -- places like West Virginia, North Dakota, Indiana, and Montana -- had no problem voting with us on those issues, and took no polling hit from doing so.

The question now is whether we will do what Democrats so often fail to do, which is to persist in the messaging wars, continuing to defend our positions, while attacking Republican policies. If we do, we will win the debate over these issues decisively, as happened in the PA-18 special election for the U.S. House seat in March. Even in a district carried by Trump by 20 points, even though the Republicans spent millions of dollars attacking Conor Lamb on the tax issue, Lamb embraced economic issues that mattered to his working-class district and won the election.

Health care and taxes will be back many times in many ways in the years ahead as big legislative fights. They both present perennial problems for governance. But there will be other big defining fights in the years to come:

1. **Social Security, Medicare, and Medicaid.** These critical programs are almost certainly going to be attacked by Republican budget-cutters. Democrats need to stand strong on these fights, and show that they are fighting not just for senior citizens, but those generations coming after them, on

these programs that help people stay out of poverty, take care of their health, and get nursing home coverage. Just because Democrats have not done well with senior voters in recent years doesn't mean we can't do a lot better, and picking a fight over these programs will go a long way in making that happen.

2. **Infrastructure.** As I wrote in Chapter 6, infrastructure is one of the most underfunded areas of national spending. Trump has promised $1.5 trillion dollars in new infrastructure funding, but the legislation he proposed was so pathetic that even Republicans laughed it off the Hill. Trump's $1.5 trillion turned out to be mainly from state and local jurisdictions, money they don't have.

Democrats should fight back with a specific, substantive proposal. As I wrote earlier, an infrastructure bank backed by a federal guarantee and funded by state and city pension funds would provide an ongoing source of money, avoiding these yearly squabbles on the Hill that all too often end in a big, fat dysfunctional nothing. Despite Trump's trademark grandiose rhetoric, Republicans on the Hill generally don't care about infrastructure and rarely want to spend more on it. Given how fundamental to creating jobs infrastructure is, this is an important battle with both symbolic and substantive implications.

3. **Energy.** More and more Americans believe that climate change is real and that humans are causing it. Given the potential number of new jobs in renewable energy, it's time to wade into this fight with glee. So long as we make it clear that we will provide a smooth transition for workers in the oil and coal industries, per what I wrote in Chapter 6, this is a great fight because it reminds people that we are the party of the future.

4. **Education.** Betsy DeVos is the best symbol of an arrogant, clueless Cabinet Secretary since Donald Rumsfeld. A fight over privatizing public schools is just the kind of fight we want to have. I say, bring it on!

The other big education fight we want to have is on college affordability. Democrats have some divisions on this issue, with different Democrats supporting a range of plans: free college for all, free public college for all, free college for those under a certain income level, and Elizabeth Warren's proposal to provide student loans at the same rate (0.01%) the Federal Reserve offered Too-Big-to-Fail banks during the financial crisis. Just like health care, when we get a majority back in both houses and the presidency, we can work through which plan we go with, but in the meantime we can pick all kinds of fights with Republicans who want to make it harder to get college loans rather than making them more accessible and affordable.

5. **Wall Street.** Democrats need to stop taking campaign cash from the big banks and then shilling for them on deregulation. What we need instead is a fight with the Republicans on Wall Street issues. This is a battle that is always good for us, both in terms of base and swing voters.

    Some Democrats get very nervous about taking on Wall Street because they get a lot of contributions from the industry. But we should enter into this fight with vigor: nothing could be more fun and more politically useful. And if it pisses off the Wall Street donors? Bernie Sanders, Elizabeth Warren, Sherrod Brown, Jeff Merkley, and many other Democrats in big races have already shown that candidates can raise enough money online and from liberal donors to give themselves the opportunity to win.

6. **Big Tech**. People love their tech toys and conveniences, but in the last couple of years, there has been a growing concern about the massive size and power of the biggest tech companies. Google and Facebook currently corner 68% of digital ad revenue. Facebook has become an utterly ad-driven company whose completely non-transparent black box of an algorithm changes constantly. Its abuse of personal data and customer privacy, as well as selling companies and the

Russians the data they used to manipulate our politics, is mind-blowing.

Amazon has a history of using its massive size to punish book publishers and other companies who cross it. Not to mention their own workers who are subject to notoriously abusive labor practices in a quest for ever-greater efficiency and profit. "Sharing economy" companies like Airbnb and Uber have created all kinds of problems for cities and neighborhoods: skyrocketing housing costs, discrimination against people of color and people with disabilities, job loss, and safety issues. (I am proud to work with a coalition of housing groups, community organizations, disability rights groups, labor, and the hotel industry on holding Airbnb accountable.) Voters generally don't like it when any company is so dominant that it can engineer these kinds of abuses of power.

7. **Money in politics.** If Trump and modern Republicanism is the ultimate in cronyism and pay-to-play, Democrats have to - after talking about it for three decades - finally take on Big Money in politics. Public financing of campaigns won't solve all of our ills regarding money in politics, but it will make a huge difference. Democratic candidates for Congress won't have to spend seven hours a day on the phone begging rich people for money. All the issues and problems listed in this entire book will be easier to solve if we don't have to constantly rely on contributions from special interests.

Donald Trump bragged about buying off politicians during his campaign; Congressional Republicans like Lindsey Graham openly admitted that they passed the recent tax cut bill at the behest of their donors; and don't forget about Mick Mulvaney and the CFPB. Democrats can use this behavior as fuel to the fire to raise the money-in-politics issue constantly, and talk about how we can solve it.

The great thing about picking these fights is that these issues matter to just about everyone. Everyone cares about the quality of their roads, bridges, and highways. Everyone consumes energy. Just about everyone's kids go to school, and if they don't, their lives are affected by the consequences of an under-resourced public education system. Everyone has to deal with the banking system. And the vast majority of people find themselves wrestling with the big tech companies in one way or another. These are not regional issues or constituency issues, they are universal issues, and if people see us fighting on their behalf with the powers that be, they will be grateful.

The Fight for Equal Rights and Voting Rights

Another set of fights going back to our roots that Democrats should embrace are the fights over equal rights and voting rights. We are the party that has always pushed to expand the number of voters, all the way back to the 1790s. We are the party that in the 1800s and early 1900s welcomed immigrants into the country while many politicians opposed their coming, and the party that passed the Immigration and Nationality Act of 1965 that did away with racial categories in immigration. We are the party that worked with the suffragists to get women the right to vote. And we are the party that joined forces with the civil rights movement to break the back of Jim Crow by passing the Civil Rights Act of 1964 and the Voting Rights Act of 1965.

These issues, which a lot of people had assumed were long settled, have become front and center once again in this ugly decade. After Republicans gained control of state governments in the 2010 landslide, they carried out a single-minded program of voter suppression to make it far more difficult for poor people, students, and people of color to vote.

In the meantime, Donald Trump has become the most openly racist president since James Buchanan. From banning immigrants based on whether their countries had large numbers of Muslims (regardless of whether anyone from those countries had ever committed an act of terrorism) to refusing to condemn white supremacists who marched in Charlottesville, Trump has gone far beyond the clever dog-whistling politics of earlier generations of Republican politicians. He has willingly become the candidate happy to welcome the support of white supremacists everywhere. And this is not just "Trump being Trump," saying random stupid things. His administration's policies and appointees very much reflect a racist approach to governing.

It isn't just racism either. Trump's sexism goes well beyond sexually assaulting women and then bragging about it. This administration on issue after issue, and appointment after appointment, has shown that they want to lessen women's power and personal agency.

As the party of equality and democracy, we need to proudly fight all these battles. This is a fundamental part of being the party of the people: that we stand for all the people, all the time. And the voters are with us on these issues, with majorities clearly in favor of comprehensive immigration reform, criminal justice reform, abortion rights, LGBT rights, voting rights, and a wide variety of other social justice concerns. So long as we are also talking about the economy, we have no political problem doing what Democrats should do – stand tall as the party of fairness.

An Old-Fashioned Word with a Powerful Meaning

No one uses the word pluralism much anymore, but it is a profoundly important concept that was central to those early debates about democracy in our country's beginning days. To the founders, democracy could not exist without pluralism, which they defined as a system where no one faction, industry, region, or political office had too much power. A lot of historians have focused on the idea of checks and balances and separation of powers in terms of the government structure itself, but pluralism meant much more than that. Founders like Franklin, George Mason, Jefferson, and Madison wanted distributed power: no city or state or region, no industry or single company, should have enough power that they could dominate all the others.

Maybe the word is too old and dull to revive, but the idea is not. Democrats need to fight for more power to those who have too little, in order to be a check on the massive power being accumulated by a few. No industry should be able to dominate the economy; no single company should be able to dominate an industry or a market; no small collection of big donors should be able to dominate our political system. Workers and consumers should have more power to negotiate on more equal terms with the companies that employ and sell to them. And small business people should not have to compete against monopolies or oligopolies.

It's as simple as that, and it goes to the core of being the party of the people again. We need to be the party that gives strength to those who are fighting forces with too much power -- in our economy or in our government.

Courage, and Finding Our Identity Again

Democrats, we can get our identity back, and with it, our mojo for winning elections. We must go back to truly being the party of the people again, the party of working people. The party of small business instead of monopolists. The party of equality and democracy instead of the party of the elites. The party of the small online contributions rather than the one of seven-figure checks.

What we need is what the Cowardly Lion asked for in The Wizard of Oz, courage. And just like the Cowardly Lion found his courage again in the fight to save that girl from the heartland, we can find courage again in the fights we take on for working people.

We need to show the courage to take on the big money interests that are distorting our economy and our democracy. The conventional wisdom says that we can't afford to take on Big Money, but we have already proven we can – if we are bold enough to inspire people.

In 2012, Elizabeth Warren was running against an extremely well-funded incumbent, and the denizens of Wall Street were determined to beat her. She proceeded to raise more than $20 million in small contributions, more than any other Senate candidate by far and more than her opponent, and won going away. Meanwhile, Sherrod Brown, the progressive populist firebrand from Ohio, had more money spent against him than any Senate candidate in history, but he won going away -- and sadly is still the only Democratic statewide candidate to win Ohio since 2008. Tammy Baldwin ran a fiery progressive populist campaign, and raised enough money to beat a well-financed popular former governor in Wisconsin.

Flash forward to 2016. Bernie Sanders, taking on the most dominant, heavily favored non-incumbent frontrunner for either party in modern American history, took no money from wealthy donors and held no fundraisers. He ended up raising over $229,000,000, plenty of money to run a competitive campaign, as he competed in every state all the way to the end. More than 95% of his money came from small-dollar, online donations.

If our candidates have a bold, courageous platform that they demonstrably fight for, we can inspire voters and raise the money we need to win big elections. But we also need courage against the pundits and purveyors of Beltway conventional wisdom. They describe progressive populism as the kind of liberalism that can't win, despite all the candidates in swing states and tough races who have won in recent years, despite Bernie still being the most popular politician in America according to most public polling. And, I might add, despite Trump running a populist campaign railing against Wall Street, trade deals, the global elite, and big money in politics.

D.C. conventional wisdom is almost always wrong, and so is what I call 'D.C. centrism.' D.C. centrism is entirely unrelated to what voters in the real America would think of as centrism. It is the idea that Democrats would somehow become more popular if they supported things that most voters hate. The D.C. centrists' favorite policy idea is cutting Social Security and Medicare for the sake of "fiscal responsibility," despite the fact that those are the most popular programs in America. These D.C. centrists would be appalled if Democrats became the party of the people again. We need to have the courage to ignore them.

D.C. centrism also worships at the altar of bipartisanship regardless of the policy results. Unfortunately, history shows that many of the best laws that have ever been passed were either entirely or overwhelmingly achieved by Democrats alone (or if you want to go way back to the 1860s, by Republicans -- the progressive party of the time -- alone). In recent years, with big money so dominant and the Republicans having moved so far to the right, pretty much everything passed with bipartisan support was a sop to big corporate special interests or bad conservative ideas. Trade deals, welfare reform, Three Strikes and You're Out laws, the Telecom Act of 1996, and the Wall Street deregulation bill of 1999 were all bipartisan and they were all bad for working families.

Instead of bipartisan bad ideas, Democrats should stick to their principles and fight for things that truly help people. It has always been a strange thing to me that some Democrats don't like to fight on issues where we hold the high political ground. These days when I go up to Capitol Hill and talk strategy with Senators and House members, where I think Democrats go most wrong is the lack of courage and confidence that the people will stay with us. On the DACA fight, for example, polling showed that more than 80% of voters were with us on the issue, and more than 60% on the immigration issue in general. But when the showdown came on the issue in the government shutdown fight, we stood tall for a weekend and then turned tail and ran. After a confusing weekend of muddled messaging (some Democrats said we were shutting the government for the Dreamers, some said it was something else), too many Democrats thought people would get mad at us if we held out, even though we had won every shutdown fight of the last 25 years (voters always end up blaming Republicans, the party that hates government, for government shutdowns).

The fights we pick, and even more importantly sustain, will determine how voters think about us. We need to rebuild our identity as the party of the people, brick by brick. We need to fight for working people, for fairness, for the future, and for freedom as we define it. When we make those fights of the people our own, when we sustain the battle rather than giving up when it looks tough, we will reclaim our history and our soul as the party of the people. When that happens, we will start winning elections again, not just once in a while when there is an unpopular Republican president, but consistently over a generation.

The good news is this: voters like courage. They like boldness and big ideas that shake things up. They like authenticity. They like rejecting the conventional wisdom.

Democrats, it is time to return to our roots and reclaim our identity. The Democratic Party's fundamental mission has always been to fight for the people, all of the people. Our party's founders wrote the Declaration of Independence and the Bill of Rights. We have always fought for expanding voting rights, for more people getting educated, and for our economy to be oriented toward the everyday working people who make this country run. If we claim this identity again and hold it close to our hearts, we will survive the era of Trump and this ugly moment in American history. It is always darkest before the dawn, but the dawn is indeed coming.

POSTSCRIPT

A decade ago, the economy was in full-scale meltdown. Politicians from both parties had deregulated Wall Street and let the financial industry run roughshod over the rest of us. The result was an economic panic dramatically worse than any in 80 years, with millions of jobs lost, millions of bankruptcies, millions of homes in foreclosure. And when the crisis hit, the perpetrators of the financial fraud that had caused this misery were bailed out, rather than prosecuted. And then those same bankers ended up getting record bonuses the year after the crisis had peaked.

Nancy Pelosi and Harry Reid had the good sense to appoint a little-known professor named Elizabeth Warren to head a small agency whose job was to oversee the Troubled Asset Relief Program (TARP), a fund established to bail out the Too-Big-to-Fail banks. When Warren ignored conventional wisdom and bucked her own party to challenge Obama Treasury Secretary Tim Geithner on how he was spending TARP dollars, she electrified the activists following the issue. She later pushed to get a new agency, the Consumer Financial Protection Bureau, included in the Dodd-Frank financial reform bill. When politicians from both parties were trying to get her to back down -- I was being told by the White House and Harry Reid's office that Senate Banking Committee Chair Chris Dodd didn't want to include CFPB in the bill -- she kept fighting. At the time, Warren told a reporter from the Huffington Post, "My first choice is a strong consumer agency. My second choice is no agency at all and plenty of blood and teeth left on the floor...My 99th choice is some mouthful of mush that doesn't get the job done." And by not backing down, she won the day, and a strong CFPB made it into the bill. The result of fighting these battles in the way she did made her a national hero.

Her Senator, Scott Brown, had been a close ally to Wall Street when the Dodd-Frank bill was being debated, supporting the bill but only at the cost of weakening it considerably. He was a moderate, charismatic, popular, extremely well-funded senator with a savvy campaign team. None of the longtime Democratic politicians in Massachusetts wanted to take him on in his re-election battle in 2012, so Warren decided to run. She went on to become the only challenger to beat an incumbent senator that year, outraising Brown's huge campaign war chest with the massive surge of small, online donations she received.

The next cycle, in 2014, the Washington Post reported on focus groups of swing voters in the Denver suburbs who were completely unenthused with either party's frontrunners, but a lot of whom spoke favorably of the freshman Senator from Massachusetts. They liked her because she had the courage to take on Wall Street and fight for what she believed in.

I tell this story because Democrats need to do more of what Warren did: show their independence by fighting the powers that be for what they think is right. The American people are tired of business as usual, they are unhappy with both political parties and the D.C. establishment, but they respond instinctively to the people whom they think will shake things up and fight for their interests. They want political leaders who will "leave blood and teeth on the floor" in fighting for working people, and who will challenge their own party's leaders if necessary to get things done for them.

Here's another story that in some ways is even more important, because it is about regular folks fighting the good fight, and winning. In states dominated by Republicans, public school teachers are treated like shit -- there's just no other way to describe it. Their pay is low; their pensions have been vastly underfunded and are running out of money; the schools they are supposed to teach children in are falling apart; they have out-of-date textbooks; their classrooms are over-crowded. And these teachers have had enough. In West Virginia, teachers launched a statewide strike. Instead of the public turning on them, they got massive support and sympathy from parents who knew that their kids were being mistreated, too. Republican legislators tried to ignore them and hoped they would give up and go away. But the teachers kept the strike alive until legislators finally granted some of their demands.

West Virginia teachers sparked a wildfire. In Oklahoma, Kentucky, and Arizona, teachers went on strike as well. By the time this book is published, there will almost certainly be more states where teachers launch strikes. In every state, Republican politicians talked down to them and dismissed them. But the teachers held strong, and are winning big gains. This is all happening literally as I write, so I don't know what will happen next, but the fight goes on.

This kind of fighting spirit is especially urgent in the age of Trump and Trumpism, when our opposition is ruthless and the power of money is immense. Our opponents are happy to demonize entire races and religions to win, happy to keep people from voting because of their age, income, and race. Our opponents have no trouble lying about any fact to keep in power. Our opponents want to repeal all of the progress of the 20th century and leave individual citizens at the mercy of giant corporations with no checks on their power.

But contrary to conventional wisdom, this is not a post-truth era. If we fight the good fight, if we stand shoulder-to-shoulder with the people and go toe-to-toe with the foes of democracy, the truth will come out. If we organize, friend to friend and neighbor to neighbor, our message will be heard. Our party needs to rediscover its roots and its soul. We need to remember how progressive warriors fought throughout history to build a nation dedicated to freedom, fairness, and a better future for the generations that follow. If we return to being the party of the people, we will start winning elections again. It really is as simple as that. And if we start improving the lives of regular folks in a tangible way that they can see and feel, we can heal this nation, reap the benefits for generations to come, and build a new progressive future.

BIBLIOGRAPHY

Introduction

Boyd, Bret. "Urbanization and the Mass Movement of People to Cities." Grayline Group, 25 Apr. 2018, graylinegroup.com/urbanization-catalyst-overview/.

Cohn, D'Vera, and Andrea Caumont. "10 Demographic Trends That Are Shaping the U.S. and the World." Pew Research Center, 31 Mar. 2016, www.pewresearch.org/fact-tank/2016/03/31/10-demographic-trends-that-are-shaping-the-u-s-and-the-world/.

"Daily Kos Elections Post-Nov. 8 2016 D-vs.-R Special Elections vs. Presidential Results."

Davidson, Justin. "Cities Vs. Trump." New York Magazine, 18 Apr. 2017.

Fowler, Donnie. "Reviewing Election 2016 & Finding The Democratic Path Forward." Medium, 23 Dec. 2016, medium.com/@dfowler/reviewing-election-2016-finding-the-democratic-path-forward-fe2d8d4d14a7.

Jones, Jeffrey M. "Americans Hold Record Liberal Views on Most Moral Issues." Gallup, 11 May 2017, news.gallup.com/poll/210542/americans-hold-record-liberal-views-moral-issues.aspx.

Kiersz, Andy. "How Americans Really Feel about Their Country on 33 Key Issues, and How That Has Changed over 40 Years." Business Insider, 25 Feb. 2017, www.businessinsider.com/american-public-opinion-on-major-issues-institutions-2017-2.

Leip, David. "Dave Leip's Atlas of U.S. Presidential Elections." 1974 Gubernatorial General Election Results - Alabama, uselectionatlas.org/RESULTS/index.html.

"Partisan Composition of State Legislatures 2002-2014." National Conference of State Legislatures, www.ncsl.org/.

"Party Divisions of the House of Representatives*." US House of Representatives: History, Art & Archives, history.house.gov/Institution/Party-Divisions/Party-Divisions/.

"Party Division." U.S. Senate: Select Committee on Presidential Campaign Activities, 19 Jan. 2017, www.senate.gov/history/partydiv.htm.

"PROFILE AMERICA FACTS FOR FEATURES: CB16-FF.18." U.S. Census Bureau, 25 Aug. 2016, www.census.gov/content/dam/Census/newsroom/facts-for-features/2016/CB16-FF.18.pdf.

"State Legislative Elections, 2018." Ballotpedia, ballotpedia.org/State_legislative_elections,_2018.

"STATE PARTISAN COMPOSITION." National Conference of State Legislatures, 11 Apr. 2018, www.ncsl.org/research/about-state-legislatures/partisan-composition.aspx.

"U.S. Governors - Number by Political Party Affiliation 1990-2017 | Statistic." Statista, www.statista.com/statistics/198486/number-of-governors-in-the-us-by-political-party-affiliation/.

"U.S. Governors - Number by Political Party Affiliation 1990-2017 | Statistic." Statista, www.statista.com/statistics/198486/number-of-governors-in-the-us-by-political-party-affiliation/.

Wilson, Reid. "Dems Hit New Low in State Legislatures." The Hill, 18 Nov. 2016, thehill.com/homenews/campaign/306736-dems-hit-new-low-in-state-legislatures.

Chapter 1

Devine, Christopher J., and Kyle C. Kopko. "5 Things You Need to Know about How Third-Party Candidates Did in 2016." The Washington Post, 15 Nov. 2016, www.washingtonpost.com/news/monkey-cage/wp/2016/11/15/5-things-you-need-to-know-about-how-third-party-candidates-did-in-2016/?utm_term=.4d226dd200a2.

Dougherty, Conor. "Boom and Gloom: An Economic Warning for California." The New York Times, 13 Feb. 2018, www.nytimes.com/2018/02/13/business/economy/california-recession.html.

Gallup, Inc. "Presidential Approval Ratings -- Barack Obama." Gallup.com, news.gallup.com/poll/116479/barack-obama-presidential-job-approval.aspx.

Greenberg, Stanley. "The Democrats' 'Working-Class Problem.'" The American Prospect, 1 June 2017, prospect.org/article/democrats'-'working-class-problem'.

Le Miere, Jason. "BERNIE SANDERS VOTERS HELPED TRUMP WIN AND HERE'S PROOF." Newsweek, 23 Aug. 2017, www.newsweek.com/bernie-sanders-trump-2016-election-654320.

Lynch, Mounir. "Whaley to Focus on Opioid Epidemic, Job Growth." The News Record, 5 Oct. 2017, www.newsrecord.org/news/whaley-to-focus-on-opioid-epidemic-job-growth/article_d28b18a2-a8a0-11e7-a449-3b38254c912f.html.

Omero, Margie. "Wall Street, Bush, and Obama: Enough Blame to Go around?" Huffpost, 6 Dec. 2016, www.huffingtonpost.com/margie-omero/wall-street-bush-and-obam_b_1024044.html.

Russo, John. "Have Ohio Democrats Learned Anything About the Working Class?" The American Prospect, 2 Mar. 2018, prospect.org/article/have-ohio-democrats-learned-anything-about-working-class.

Chapter 2

Burnett, Bob. "Indivisible: A Social Action Startup for Democracy." Common Dreams, 10 Mar. 2017, www.commondreams.org/views/2017/03/10/indivisible-social-action-startup-democracy.

Debenedetti, Gabriel. "Obama's Party-Building Legacy Splits Democrats." Politico, 9 Feb. 2017, www.politico.com/story/2017/02/obama-democrats-party-building-234820.

Chapter 3

Badger, Emily. "https://Www.nytimes.com/2016/11/21/Upshot/as-American-as-Apple-Pie-the-Rural-Votes-Disproportionate-Slice-of-Power.html ." The New York Times, 20 Nov. 2016, www.nytimes.com/2016/11/21/upshot/as-american-as-apple-pie-the-rural-votes-disproportionate-slice-of-power.html .

Begley, Sarah. "Hillary Clinton Leads by 2.8 Million in Final Popular Vote Count." Time Magazine, 20 Dec. 2016, time.com/4608555/hillary-clinton-popular-vote-final/.

Brownstein, Ronald. "How the Rustbelt Paved Trump's Road to Victory." The Atlantic, 10 Nov. 2016, www.theatlantic.com/politics/archive/2016/11/trumps-road-to-victory/507203/.
Cheung, Kylie. "Why Do Single Women Have Such Low Voter Turnout Rates?" Mediaite, 27 July 2017, www.mediaite.com/online/why-do-single-women-have-such-low-voter-turnout-rates/.
"Election Polls -- Vote by Groups, 1992-1996." Gallup, news.gallup.com/poll/9466/election-polls-vote-groups-19921996.aspx.

"Exit Polls." CNN, 23 Nov. 2016, www.cnn.com/election/2016/results/exit-polls.

Gerber, Alan, et al. "Does Church Attendance Cause People to Vote? Using Blue Laws Repeal to Estimate the Effect of Religiosity on Voter Turnout." 2008, doi:10.3386/w14303.

Griffin, Rob, et al. "Voter Trends in 2016: A Final Examination." Center for American Progress, 1 Dec. 2017, www.americanprogress.org/issues/democracy/reports/2017/11/0 1/441926/voter-trends-in-2016/.

Heimlich, Russell. "Who Votes, Who Doesn't, and Why." Pew Research Center for the People and the Press, 18 Oct. 2006, www.people-press.org/2006/10/18/who-votes-who-doesnt-and-why/.

"Historical Election Results." National Archives and Records Administration, National Archives and Records Administration, www.archives.gov/federal-register/electoral-college/scores2.html#2016.

"How Groups Voted in 2008." Roper Center, ropercenter.cornell.edu/polls/us-elections/how-groups-voted/how-groups-voted-2008/.

"How Groups Voted in 2012." Roper Center, ropercenter.cornell.edu/polls/us-elections/how-groups-voted/how-groups-voted-2012/.

Katz, Celeste. "New Study Projects Stunning Drop in 2018 Millennial Voter Turnout in Battleground States." Mic, 20 July 2017, mic.com/articles/182592/new-study-projects-stunning-drop-in-2018-millennial-voter-turnout-in-battleground-states#.DNKgVm69X.

Kiersz, Andy. "How Americans Really Feel about Their Country on 33 Key Issues, and How That Has Changed over 40 Years." Business Insider, 25 Feb. 2017, www.businessinsider.com/american-public-opinion-on-major-issues-institutions-2017-2.

Krogstad, Jens Manuel, and Mark Hugo Lopez. "Black Voter Turnout Fell in 2016, Even as a Record Number of Americans Cast Ballots." Pew Research Center, 12 May 2017, www.pewresearch.org/fact-tank/2017/05/12/black-voter-turnout-fell-in-2016-even-as-a-record-number-of-americans-cast-ballots/.

Kurtzleben, Danielle. "Rural Voters Played A Big Part In Helping Trump Defeat Clinton." NPR, 14 Nov. 2016, www.npr.org/2016/11/14/501737150/rural-voters-played-a-big-part-in-helping-trump-defeat-clinton.

López, Ian Haney, et al. "Democrats Can Win by Tackling Race and Class Together. Here's Proof." The Guardian, Guardian News and Media, 14 Apr. 2018, www.theguardian.com/commentisfree/2018/apr/14/democrats-race-class-divide-2018-midterms.

Phillips, Steve. Brown Is the New White: How the Demographic Revolution Has Created a New American Majority. The New Press, 2018.

Phillips, Steve. "How to Build a Democratic Majority That Lasts." The New York Times, 5 Oct. 2016, www.nytimes.com/2016/10/05/opinion/campaign-stops/how-to-build-a-democratic-majority-that-lasts.html.

Schoffstall, Joe. "$40 Million Has Been Spent In Georgia's Record-Breaking Special Election." Washington Free Beacon, 16 June 2017, freebeacon.com/issues/40-million-spent-georgias-record-breaking-special-election/.

Schulman, Michael. "Generation LGBTQIA." The New York Times, The New York Times, 9 Jan. 2013, www.nytimes.com/2013/01/10/fashion/generation-lgbtqia.html.

"U.S. Household Income Distribution." Statista, www.statista.com/statistics/203183/percentage-distribution-of-household-income-in-the-us/.

"Voter Turnout Demographics." United States Elections Project, www.electproject.org/home/voter-turnout/demographics.

Chapter 4

"2012 Census Highlights." USDA - NASS, Census of Agriculture - Publications - 2012 - Highlights, www.agcensus.usda.gov/Publications/2012/Online_Resources/Highlights/Farm_Demographics/#how_many.

Bishop, Bill. "Finding High, Low Pay in Rural America." Rural News and Information, 24 Jan. 2011, www.dailyyonder.com/finding-high-low-pay-rural-america/2011/01/24/3131/.

CBS News. "The Digital Divide between Rural and Urban Americas Access to Internet." CBS News, CBS Interactive, 4 Aug. 2017, www.cbsnews.com/news/rural-areas-internet-access-dawsonville-georgia/.

Igielnick, Ruth. "Rural and Urban Gun Owners Have Different Experiences, Views on Gun Policy." Pew Research Center, www.pewresearch.org/fact-tank/2017/07/10/rural-and-urban-gun-owners-have-different-experiences-views-on-gun-policy/.

Parker, Kim, et al. "5. Views on Gun Policy." Pew Research Center's Social & Demographic Trends Project, 22 June 2017, www.pewsocialtrends.org/2017/06/22/views-on-gun-policy/.

Rhodan, Maya. "Heroin Abuse: White House Taps Tom Vilsack to Fight Opioids." Time, Time, 8 Feb. 2016, time.com/4211759/white-house-opioids-tom-vilsack/.

Runge, Robin. "Addressing the Access to Justice Crisis in Rural America." American Bar Association, vol. 40, no. 3, www.americanbar.org/publications/human_rights_magazine_home/2014_vol_40/vol_40_no_3_poverty/access_justice_rural_america.html.

Runyon, Luke. "Why Is The Opioid Epidemic Hitting Rural America Especially Hard?" NPR Illinois, nprillinois.org/post/why-opioid-epidemic-hitting-rural-america-especially-hard#stream/0.

"Rural Health Care Still Subpar for Most Quality Measures, Data Show." AHRQ--Agency for Healthcare Research and Quality: Advancing Excellence in Health Care, U.S. HHS: Agency for Healthcare Research and Quality, 13 Oct. 2015, www.ahrq.gov/news/newsletters/e-newsletter/490.html#1.

Searing, Adam. "Study Documents How Medicaid Expansion Helps Keep Rural Hospitals Open." Georgetown University Health Policy Institute Center For Children and Families, 12 Jan. 2018, ccf.georgetown.edu/2018/01/12/study-documents-how-medicaid-expansion-helps-keep-rural-hospitals-open/.

Semuels, Alana. "Good School, Rich School; Bad School, Poor School." The Atlantic, Atlantic Media Company, 25 Aug. 2016, www.theatlantic.com/business/archive/2016/08/property-taxes-and-unequal-schools/497333/.

"The Divide Between Rural and Urban America, in 6 Charts." U.S. News & World Report, U.S. News & World Report, www.usnews.com/news/national-news/articles/2017-03-20/6-charts-that-illustrate-the-divide-between-rural-and-urban-america.

Thiede, Brian. "6 Charts That Illustrate the Divide between Rural and Urban America." PBS, Public Broadcasting Service, 17 Mar. 2017, www.pbs.org/newshour/nation/six-charts-illustrate-divide-rural-urban-america.

Tieken, Mara Casey. "Opinion | There's a Big Part of Rural America That Everyone's Ignoring." The Washington Post, WP Company, 24 Mar. 2017, www.washingtonpost.com/opinions/theres-a-big-part-of-rural-america-that-everyones-ignoring/2017/03/24/d06d24d0-1010-11e7-ab07-07d9f521f6b5_story.html?utm_term=.95bffe4a286c.

"U.S. Census Bureau QuickFacts: Nebraska." www.census.gov/quickfacts/NE.

U.S. Census Bureau QuickFacts: Hall County, Nebraska; Nebraska. www.census.gov/quickfacts/fact/table/hallcountynebraska,NE/P ST045217.

U.S. Census Bureau QuickFacts: Scotts Bluff County, Nebraska. www.census.gov/quickfacts/fact/table/scottsbluffcountynebraska /PST045216.

Vilsack, Tom. "New Markets, New Opportunities: Strengthening Local Food Systems and Organic Agriculture." Medium, Augmenting Humanity, 4 Apr. 2016, medium.com/usda-results/new-markets-new-opportunities-strengthening-local-food-systems-and-organic-agriculture-17b529c5ea90.

Wang, Tova. "Ensuring Access to the Ballot for American Indians & Alaska Natives: New Solutions to Strengthen American Democracy." Demos IHS Report, www.demos.org/sites/default/files/publications/IHS Report-Demos.pdf.

Chapter 5

Douglas, Danielle. "Holder Concerned Megabanks Too Big to Jail." The Washington Post, WP Company, 6 Mar. 2013, www.washingtonpost.com/business/economy/holder-concerned-megabanks-too-big-to-jail/2013/03/06/6fa2b07a-869e-11e2-999e-5f8e0410cb9d_story.html?utm_term=.42d79ed2420d.

Hanley, Steve. "JOB GROWTH IN SOLAR AND RENEWABLE ENERGY SECTOR OUTPACES FOSSIL FUELS." Gas2, 5 June 2016, gas2.org/2016/06/05/job-growth-solar-renewable-energy-sector-fossil-fuels/.

Krantz, Matt. "Trump's Turn? Republican Presidents Rule Recessions." USA Today, Gannett Satellite Information Network, 20 Nov. 2016, www.usatoday.com/story/money/markets/2016/11/20/trumps-turn-republican-presidents-rule-recessions/93976832/.

Lux, Mike. "An Economy Working Only for a Few." The Huffington Post, TheHuffingtonPost.com, 21 Sept. 2013, www.huffingtonpost.com/mike-lux/an-economy-working-only-f_b_3636335.html.

Lynn, Barry C. Cornered: the New Monopoly Capitalism and the Economics of Destruction. John Wiley & Sons, 2010.

Memoli, Michael A. "Hillary Clinton Once Called TPP the 'Gold Standard.' Here's Why, and What She Says about the Trade Deal Now." Los Angeles Times, Los Angeles Times, 26 Sept. 2016, www.latimes.com/politics/la-na-pol-trade-tpp-20160926-snap-story.html.

"Obama's Not as Tough on Mergers as You Think." CNNMoney, Cable News Network, money.cnn.com/2016/04/08/news/obama-mergers-antitrust/index.html.
Popovich, Nadja. "Today's Energy Jobs Are in Solar, Not Coal." The New York Times, The New York Times, 25 Apr. 2017, www.nytimes.com/interactive/2017/04/25/climate/todays-energy-jobs-are-in-solar-not-coal.html.

Vlastelica, Ryan. "Should Trump Expect a Recession? Every Republican since Teddy Roosevelt Has Had One in Their First Term." MarketWatch, MarketWatch, 4 May 2018, www.marketwatch.com/story/should-markets-expect-a-recession-every-republican-since-teddy-roosevelt-has-had-one-in-their-first-term-2018-05-02.

Warren, Elizabeth. "Speech to Open Markets." America's Monopoly Moment | Work, Innovation, and Control in an Age of Concentrated Power. 6 Dec. 2017, Washington, DC, The Liaison Capitol Hill Hotel.

Chapter 6

Balara, Victoria. "Fox News Poll: 83 Percent Support Pathway to Citizenship for Illegal Immigrants." Fox News, FOX News Network, 28 Sept. 2017, www.foxnews.com/politics/2017/09/28/fox-news-poll-83-percent-support-pathway-to-citizenship-for-illegal-immigrants.html.

Bump, Philip. "Analysis | What the Pennsylvania Special Election Tells Us about the Democratic Turnout Surge." The Washington Post, WP Company, 14 Mar. 2018, www.washingtonpost.com/news/politics/wp/2018/03/14/what-the-pennsylvania-special-election-tells-us-about-the-democratic-turnout-surge/?utm_term=.2c1bcad645a6.

Chenoweth, Erica, and Jeremy Pressman. "Analysis | This Is What We Learned by Counting the Women's Marches." The Washington Post, WP Company, 7 Feb. 2017, www.washingtonpost.com/news/monkey-cage/wp/2017/02/07/this-is-what-we-learned-by-counting-the-womens-marches/?utm_term=.56baccdfc1da.

"Democrats vs. Republicans." PollingReport.com, www.pollingreport.com/dvsr.htm.

Greenberg, Stanley. "The Average Joe's Proviso." Washington Monthly, 18 May 2016, washingtonmonthly.com/magazine/junejulyaug-2015/the-average-joes-proviso/.

Hoium, Travis. "Renewable Energy Is Now Unstoppable." The Motley Fool, The Motley Fool, 19 Nov. 2017, www.fool.com/investing/2017/11/19/renewable-energy-is-now-cheaper-than-fossil-fuels.aspx.

Matthews, Dylan. "The Republican Tax Bill Got Worse: Now the Top 1% Gets 83% of the Gains." Vox, Vox, 18 Dec. 2017, www.vox.com/policy-and-politics/2017/12/18/16791174/republican-tax-bill-congress-conference-tax-policy-center.

Moore, David W. "Majority of Americans Prefer Path to Citizenship for Illegal Immigrants." Gallup, 11 Apr. 2006, news.gallup.com/poll/22327/majority-americans-prefer-path-citizenship-illegal-immigrants.aspx.

Schumacher, Mary. "Here's Why There Has Never Been a Death From Cannabis Overdose." Alternet, 9 Mar. 2018, www.alternet.org/drugs/here-why-there-has-never-been-death-cannabis-marijuana-overdose.

Stewart, Emily. "Mick Mulvaney Says in Congress, He Only Talked to Lobbyists Who Gave Him Money." Vox, Vox, 25 Apr. 2018, www.vox.com/policy-and-politics/2018/4/25/17279244/mick-mulvaney-cfpb-lobbyist-donations-banks.

Tanden, Neera, et al. "Toward a Marshall Plan for America." Center for American Progress, www.americanprogress.org/issues/economy/reports/2017/05/16/432499/toward-marshall-plan-america/.

Wallace, Tim, and Alicia Parlapiano. "Crowd Scientists Say Women's March in Washington Had 3 Times as Many People as Trump's Inauguration." The New York Times, The New York Times, 22 Jan. 2017, www.nytimes.com/interactive/2017/01/22/us/politics/womens-march-trump-crowd-estimates.html.

Wilson, Reid. "Why Democrats Keep Winning Special Elections." TheHill, The Hill, 21 Jan. 2018, thehill.com/homenews/campaign/369847-why-democrats-keep-winning-special-elections.

Windsor, Lauren. "Exclusive: Inside the Koch Brothers' Secret Billionaire Summit." The Nation, 29 June 2015, www.thenation.com/article/exclusive-behind-koch-brothers-secret-billionaire-summit/.

Chapter 7

Jeffery, Clara, and Monika Bauerlein. "The Job Killers." Mother Jones, 25 June 2017, www.motherjones.com/politics/2011/10/republicans-job-creation-kill/.

Windsor, Lauren. "Exclusive: Inside the Koch Brothers' Secret Billionaire Summit." The Nation, 29 June 2015, www.thenation.com/article/exclusive-behind-koch-brothers-secret-billionaire-summit/.

Chapter 8

"Bernie 2016 Case Study." Revolution Messaging, revolutionmessaging.com/cases/bernie-2016.

De Pinto, Jennifer, et al. "Most Americans Support DACA, but Oppose Border Wall - CBS News Poll." CBS News, CBS Interactive, 18 Jan. 2018, www.cbsnews.com/news/most-americans-support-daca-but-oppose-border-wall-cbs-news-poll/.

"Founders Online: From Alexander Hamilton to Rufus King, 3 June 1802." National Archives and Records Administration, National Archives and Records Administration, founders.archives.gov/documents/Hamilton/01-26-02-0001-0011.

"Founders Online: From John Adams to James Sullivan, 26 May 1776." National Archives and Records Administration, National Archives and Records Administration, founders.archives.gov/documents/Adams/06-04-02-0091.

"Immigration." PollingReport.com, www.pollingreport.com/immigration.htm.
Ovide, Shira. "Google and Facebook Divide Up Your Eyeballs." Bloomberg.com, Bloomberg, 21 Nov. 2016, www.bloomberg.com/gadfly/articles/2016-11-21/google-and-facebook-divide-up-your-advertising-viewing.

"Rep. Elizabeth Warren - Massachusetts District S1."
OpenSecrets, www.opensecrets.org/members-of-
congress/elections?cid=N00033492&cycle=2014.

Saad, Lydia. "Global Warming Concern at Three-Decade
High in U.S." Gallup, 14 Mar. 2017,
news.gallup.com/poll/206030/global-warming-concern-three-
decade-high.aspx.

Sherman, Erik. "Infrastructure Spending Will Be Difficult
With Massive State And Local Debt." Forbes, Forbes Magazine, 18
Feb. 2018,
www.forbes.com/sites/eriksherman/2018/02/17/infrastructure-
spending-will-be-difficult-with-massive-state-and-local-
debt/#5ea6d0696c9c.

"Summary Data for Bernie Sanders, 2016 Cycle."
OpenSecrets,
www.opensecrets.org/pres16/candidate.php?id=N00000528.

Postscript

Balz, Dan. "A Signal of Distaste for Dynasties Bodes Ill for
Bush, Clinton." The Washington Post, WP Company, 10 Jan. 2015,
www.washingtonpost.com/politics/a-signal-of-distaste-for-
dynasties-bodes-ill-for-bush-clinton/2015/01/10/079258f2-98d3-
11e4-8385-866293322c2f_story.html?utm_term=.a1ec0021ffa0.

Warren, Elizabeth. A Fighting Chance. Scribe Publications,
2015.

INDEX

older voters, 38–39
O'Neill, Tip, 18
Open Markets Institute, 68
opioid crisis, 11, 51, 59, 84–85
Organizing for America (OFA), 21
Ossoff, Jon, 41
Our Minnesota Future, viii–ix

P
PACs. See Political Action Committees (PACs)
Palnick, Laura, 52
Paris Climate Agreement, xiv
Patient Protection and Affordable Care Act. See Affordable Care Act (ACA)
PCCC. See Progressive Change Campaign Committee (PCCC)
peace, 95–97
Pelosi, Nancy, 4, 26, 113
Penn, Mark, 39
Pennsylvania, 9, 33, 52, 59, 104
people of color. See also African-Americans; racism
    in Alabama Senate special election of 2017, 33
    business and, 72
    central issues for, 7, 55
    in Democratic base, xiii, 6, 31–32
    demographics and, xvii
    dog whistling and, ix
    fairness and, 97
    hiring of, in Democratic Party, 26–27, 34
    identity politics and, 46–48
    increase in, 31–32
    racism and, x, 45
    in rural America, 52–53
    turnout of, in 2016 election, 32–33
    and War on Drugs, 85
    whites vs., as false choice, xxiii
people-to-people organizing, 14–16
Perriello, Tom, xxi
Phillips, Steve, 31–35
pluralism, 109–110
Podesta, John, xi

ABOUT THE AUTHOR

Mike Lux is a co-founder of Democracy Partners, an innovative, full-service national consulting firm launched in 2011; and has been the CEO of his own consulting firm, Mike Lux Media, since 1999. Clients have included many of the most important institutions in the progressive community, including the League of Conservation Voters, Planned Parenthood, Moveon.org, the NAACP Voter Fund, Center for Community Change, DailyKos, and Democracy Alliance. He has also been featured on various news outlets, including CNN, MSNBC, and the Thom Hartmann show; as well as being a frequent front-page contributor to The Huffington Post and regular blogger at DailyKos and Crooks & Liars.

Mike served as a senior staffer or advisor on six different presidential campaigns. He was the national constituency director for the 1992 Clinton campaign and the special assistant to the president for public liaison in the Clinton White House from 1993-1995. During his time in the Clinton Administration, Mike worked closely with a wide range of constituency groups, as well as on health care and budget issues. He served in the 1992 campaign war room, the 1993 budget war room, and the 1994 health care war room, being one of only two people to serve in all three. In the late 1990's, Mike was the senior vice-president for political action at People For the American Way and the PFAW Foundation. A member of the Obama-Biden transition team in 2008-2009, Mike was its liaison to the progressive community.

Mike currently serves on the boards of several important organizations, including the Arca Foundation and Netroots Nation, and is also a co-founder of the Center for American Progress, the Ballot Initiative Strategy Center, Progressive Majority, and Women's Voices/Women Vote. He is the chair of the board of Progressive Caucus Action Fund. Mike founded American Family Voices in 2000 and remains the chair of the board. He is also the author of the widely praised book The Progressive Revolution: How the Best in America Came to Be.

Mike Lux is a proud native of Lincoln, Nebraska, where most of his family still lives. He is married to Barbara Laur